The Inner Church is
the Hope of the World

The Inner Church is the Hope of the World

Western Esotericism as a Theology of Liberation

Nicholas Laccetti

RESOURCE *Publications* • Eugene, Oregon

THE INNER CHURCH IS THE HOPE OF THE WORLD
Western Esotericism as a Theology of Liberation

Copyright © 2018 Nicholas Laccetti. All rights reserved. Except for brief quotations in critical publications or reviews, no part of this book may be reproduced in any manner without prior written permission from the publisher. Write: Permissions, Wipf and Stock Publishers, 199 W. 8th Ave., Suite 3, Eugene, OR 97401.

Resource Publications
An Imprint of Wipf and Stock Publishers
199 W. 8th Ave., Suite 3
Eugene, OR 97401

www.wipfandstock.com

PAPERBACK ISBN: 978-1-5326-1971-7
HARDCOVER ISBN: 978-1-4982-4623-1
EBOOK ISBN: 978-1-4982-4622-4

New Revised Standard Version Bible, copyright 1989, Division of Christian Education of the National Council of the Churches of Christ in the United States of America. Used by permission. All rights reserved.

Manufactured in the U.S.A.

To my teachers, both esoteric and theologic . . .

To the Kairos Center, for being liberation theologians in action . . .

To my wife Lilly, the Sophiale of New York City . . .

To the Unknown Cadre in L. V. X.

"Perhaps I must turn my faith to the inner spiritual church, the church within the church, as the true *ekklesia* and the hope of the world."

—Rev. Dr. Martin Luther King Jr.,
  "Letter from Birmingham Jail"

". . . in another form of symbolism, the Tree is itself the elect. The blessings which are poured continually upon the outer world descend from it and from them. They are the Blessed Company in the Sanctuary of the Hidden Church. When the elect shall enter into perfect liberation, the whole world will be nourished by the Tree of Life, sustained and enlightened by SHEKINAH."

—A. E. Waite, Fellowship of the Rosy Cross,
  "Grade of Practicus"

"Let the Sons of Morning Rejoice in our Hidden Assembly, for now beginneth the fulfilment of the word of the Silver Star . . ."

—Frater Achad, "The First Golden Mesospheric"

Contents

Introduction | 1

Creation and Fall

I. The One Idea | 17
II. Social Qabalah | 26

Liberation

III. The True Grand Orient | 55
IV. The Silver Star of Bethlehem | 67

Consummation

V. The Inner Church | 83
VI. City of the Silver Star | 102

Conclusion | 131

Bibliography | 137
Index | 145

Introduction

Universal Reformation

IN 1947, PROTESTANT THEOLOGIAN Karl Barth introduced the phrase *Ecclesia semper reformanda est*—"the church is always to be reformed."[1] Barth used the phrase to express the Reformed conviction that the Christian church must constantly examine itself and continue to evolve and reform, a teaching that thinks of the Reformation as a permanent state rather than an historic event. Since the Second Vatican Council, certain radical Catholic theologians like Hans Küng have also used the saying to express their desire for a church that remains open to the world and to the spirit of the times.[2]

Yet before the Second Vatican Council, before Karl Barth, and even before the Protestant Reformation and the Catholic Counter-Reformation, there was a major philosophical, theological, and spiritual drive to reform the church. This has been called, by some, the Hermetic Reformation.[3] Its proponents saw it as a universal reformation—one that would transform all aspects of the church and European society. Rather than a return to the Bible or to traditional Christian dogmas, this reformation would be rooted in Hermetic philosophy, Renaissance Neoplatonism, and Christian Cabala—the primary sources of the Western esoteric tradition.[4]

1. Perisho, "Semper reformanda."
2. Simut, *Ontology of the Church*, 172.
3. Heiser, *Prisci Theologi and the Hermetic Reformation in the Fifteenth Century*.
4. For an overview of the concept of universal reformation in the Western

INTRODUCTION

Marsilio Ficino, through his translations of the Hermetica, Plato, and Plotinus, provided a corpus of ancient wisdom that he and other Renaissance philosophers believed to represent a *prisca theologia*, a perennial philosophy that stretched from Zoroaster and Hermes Trismegistus through Plato and Moses, all the way to Jesus Christ and the apostles. Ficino and his brilliant student, Giovanni Pico della Mirandola, thought that a return to this pristine theology would reform the Catholic Church and usher in a new golden age of utopian society, united under a philosopher-priest that some humanists saw as an enlightened role for the pope. Pico's Renaissance manifesto, the *Oration on the Dignity of Man*, suggested that the human vocation, expressed through the universal tradition of the perennial philosophy, is a mystical vocation that joins together morality, the scientific study of nature, and the regeneration of society according to eternal, divine principles.

Ficino and Pico drew on Platonism, Neoplatonism, Hermetism, and Cabala to make their arguments for the *prisca theologia* and the universal reformation of the church and society. They also practiced a form of Christian natural magic, or astral magic—the drawing down of the powers of the stars and the astrological planets into talismans and other images. Ficino even suggested that it might be possible to create "a universal image, an image of the very universe itself," in order to draw down the power of the whole macrocosm.[5] Inspired by the teachings of the hermetic text the *Asclepius*, Ficino argued that such magic was acceptable for Christians because it worked with natural, created forces rather than through the use of demonic pacts or other supernatural feats. The more conservative elements of the Roman Catholic Church were not so sure—both Ficino and Pico suffered from periods of ecclesiastical censure, as well as periods of official patronage and support. It would be the more radical doctrines of Giordano Bruno, the later Hermetist and Neoplatonist who argued for a full return to the ancient Egyptian magical religion, that would be roundly condemned

---

esoteric traditions of the early modern period, see Hall, *Orders of Universal Reformation*.

5. Ficino, *Three Books on Life*, 3.XIX.

by the militant Counter-Reformation church, leading to Bruno's execution by burning at the stake in February 1600.[6]

As readers of Frances Yates and other scholars of Hermetic philosophy know, however, the story didn't end there. The Rosicrucian Manifestos, in their own unique post-Reformation context, provided a new esoteric key for the aspiration to universal reformation, and the traditions of utopian texts like Francis Bacon's *The New Atlantis* and Tommaso Campanella's *The City of the Sun* kept alive the dream of a new universal civilization ruled by an enlightened class of philosopher-priests.[7]

In this same seventeenth-century milieu, John Amos Comenius, the Czech philosopher, pedagogue, and Moravian theologian, a correspondent of Johann Valentin Andreae (probable author of the *Chymical Wedding of Christian Rosenkreutz*), promoted the notion of pansophy or Pansophism, a program of universal education and an attempt to organize all human knowledge. Comenius's pansophic ideas prefigured the later encyclopedic movement of the eighteenth century, but were tinged with Hermetic and Rosicrucian concepts. As Manly P. Hall explains, Comenius's concept of a pansophic university

> combines the function of a college and a temple . . . The plan is Utopian in the education field. . . . Through Pansophy the human being was to be led gently and wisely through the knowledge of *things* to the love and service of God, the source of all things."[8]

The concept of Christian pansophy was linked to the utopian schemas of Bacon and Campanella, as well as to the Rosicrucianism of Andreae. One of the only previous uses of the term *Pansophia*, according to Hall, was in Frater Theophilus's Rosicrucian tract *Speculum Sophicum Rhodo-Stauroticum,* which purported to give an "extensive explanation of the *Collegium* and of the rules of

---

6. The classic account, though it is not without its modern critiques, is Yates, *Giordano Bruno and the Hermetic Tradition*.

7. Yates, *Rosicrucian Enlightenment*. See also Hall, *Orders of Universal Reformation*.

8. Hall, *Orders of Universal Reformation*, 89.

the specially enlightened Brotherhood of the Rosicrucians."[9] The *Speculum* is unique in that it contains a description of the *Collegium Fraternitatis*:

> It is a building, a great building, without doors or windows; a princely, yes, imperial palace, to be seen from everywhere and still hidden from the eyes of men. . . . It is . . . so rich, so artistically and marvelously constructed that there is no art, science, riches, gold, precious stones, money, possessions, honor, authority and knowledge in the whole world which cannot be found in this most blessed palace in the highest degree.[10]

As Hall concludes, in Theophilus's description of the *Collegium* we have "a direct reference to a Pansophic College published nineteen years prior to the outline for such an institution with the same name prepared by Comenius."[11] The pansophic college, then, as a part of the Rosicrucian mythos, is both a schema of education and the systematization of knowledge for the purposes of universal reformation, and a mystical parable about the way of return to God both for individuals and for society.

Since the Renaissance era of Ficino, Pico, and Bruno, and the Rosicrucian era of Comenius, Andreae, Campanella, and the manifestos, the *prisca theologia* has survived through the work of the esoteric orders, fraternal societies, and occult teachers of the Western esoteric tradition.[12] Yet while mentions of universal reformation are still made in various currents of Western esotericism, these are not usually programs for social reform like Comenius's pansophic college. Instead, the occult teachers and esoteric gurus make vague overtures toward a coming spiritual new age—the Era of the Holy Spirit during the French occult revival, the Age of Aquarius in America during the 1960s, or the (unfulfilled)

---

9. Ibid., 90.
10. Ibid., 90.
11. Ibid., 90.
12. For the classic overview of Western esotericism as a field of academic study, the historical periodization of Western esotericism, and summaries of its most significant schools of thought, see Faivre, *Access to Western Esotericism*.

cosmic transformation of 2012. Some orders do suggest a program of reform or revolution—the original Bavarian Illuminati supported the Enlightenment ideals of the eighteenth century, while the moral philosophy and symbolism of Freemasonry may have indirectly influenced the French and American Revolutions. And Ordo Templi Orientis, reorganized around the *Book of the Law* by the notorious magus Aleister Crowley, does hold some utopian notions of a future Thelemic society (Crowley's new religion based on his channeled texts) blossoming in force and fire during the later years of Crowley's Aeon of Horus.

But few esoteric orders do much concrete work toward organizing such a massive reformation of human religious and civic institutions as that envisioned by Pico, Bruno, or the early Rosicrucians. To put it mildly, the accumulation of the political and social power necessary for movement building is not a strong suit of occultists in general. Instead, a post-Jungian psychologizing and internalizing of esoteric doctrines has made Hermetic magic more of a gnostic pursuit of inner knowledge—or, worse, a self-help fad—rather than a cosmogonic enterprise that would radically transform the entire macrocosm through the mediation of the microcosmic human being.

Liberation Theology

In this respect, the modern iterations of the Western esoteric tradition—the secret societies, initiatory lineages, and magical orders that purport to maintain to this day the hidden knowledge announced so explosively by the first Rosicrucian Manifestos—are socially and culturally anemic compared to some of the work being done among more mainstream, and traditionally less radical, branches of Western religion, including orthodox Christianity. Since the development of the Protestant social gospel and Catholic social teaching in the early twentieth century, and the later blossoming of liberation theology across the world in the 1960s, many mainline Christian denominations (or at least their more radical fringes) have embraced the idea that religious believers

INTRODUCTION

must engage with the world and its structures in order to radically transform the socially and economically oppressive status quo. Christian liberation theologians like Gustavo Gutiérrez, Juan Luis Segundo, or James Cone would agree that the world is in need of a universal reformation, or even a universal revolution.

While studying for my Masters of Divinity degree at Union Theological Seminary in New York City, a liberal seminary focused primarily on the social gospel tradition, liberation theology, and empire-critical biblical studies, I was sometimes frustrated by the lack of emphasis on mystical approaches to the Christian theological tradition. This would include any appreciation of the Western esoteric traditions, new religious movements, or the occult. It sometimes seemed that only a materialist analysis of politics and religion was possible at Union. And yet I found myself devoting my field education internship while at Union, and my professional life now, to working for an organization that examines the power of religion for human rights and social justice, specifically the work of organizing a broad social movement to end systemic racism, poverty, militarism, and ecological destruction, inspired by the work and theology of the Rev. Dr. Martin Luther King Jr.[13]

At Union, I exulted in reading elaborate examples of philosophical and mystical theology, just as I spent most of my free time delving into obscure occult texts, but I divided that time with work for social justice, with supporting political organizing through communications and other practical skills, and with studying the history of social change within the Christian tradition. And now, as I sit down to introduce a book on the dialogue between Western esotericism and Christian theology, I find that my sources and examples of Christian theology are firmly within the tradition of liberation theology. I believe that the core of the Christian tradition is liberationist—freedom and abundance for the poor and dispossessed. The difficulty now is in seeing how these examples

---

13. This organization is the Kairos Center for Religion, Rights, and Social Justice based at Union Theological Seminary, and the movement is the Poor People's Campaign: A National Call for Moral Revival, a renewal of the 1968 Poor People's Campaign that Dr. King helped organize in the last years of his life.

INTRODUCTION

of Christian theology interact and intersect with the sources of Western esotericism, a field of interest that often brings to mind the ideas of secret knowledge, personal spiritual attainment, and elitist spiritual hierarchies—not to mention mushy new age individualism—in esotericism's more recent expressions.

It would be exhausting to merely catalogue the historical and contemporary examples of how Western esotericism has been used in the service of radical politics. Just as many, if not more, examples could be amassed for esotericism in the service of conservative politics, or in the service of an apolitical stance toward contemporary social issues. Instead, in this attempt at establishing a dialogue between Christian theology and esotericism, I will focus on two more important factors in Western esotericism and its relationship with radical social change:

1. The (esoteric) commitment to the universal reformation of the whole wide world, in the service of a new and transformed humanity, expressed more or less consistently in most examples of historic Western esotericism, though often obscured in more recent examples of the individualist and consumerist spiritualities of the new age and contemporary occultism.

2. The (theological) stance that expressions of Western esotericism represent examples of what Dorothee Sölle calls the "silent cry" and what Edward Schillebeeckx labels irruptions of the *humanum,* expressions of human yearning and hope for abundance and meaning in lives that are often marked by suffering, oppression, and meaninglessness.[14]

I will execute this dialogue between these two unlikely bedfellows—Western esotericism and Christian liberation theology—by following the basic structure of Christian salvation history: Creation and Fall, Liberation (or the salvation wrought by Jesus Christ), and Consummation (or eschatology). In the chapters to come, though my overall theological stance is guided by

14. See Sölle, *Silent Cry,* 48–49. We will examine Edward Schillebeeckx's notion of the *humanum* in detail below.

the teachings of Christian liberation theology and my work in contemporary movements to establish social justice, my sources or theological *loci* will not only be the usual suspects in a book on liberation theology, but will be the occultists, magicians, and mystics of the Western esoteric tradition. I will treat esoteric sources as genuine sources of spiritual and theological insight, and as legitimate interlocutors for more traditional theologians. If, as Gustavo Gutiérrez writes, "God is revealed in history, and it is likewise in history that persons encounter the Word made flesh"—describing a position that is shared by many proponents of the theology of liberation—then we will also encounter God, we will encounter the Word, within the particular history of human religious expressions that is Western esotericism.[15]

Pansophy and Liberation

One significant strand of the Western esoteric tradition—pansophy—would agree wholeheartedly with liberation theology that it is in history (and in nature) that we encounter God, and that it is the responsibility of the Christian to seek radical social change. Although little known in contemporary discourse outside of scholars of Western esotericism, the drive to reform all of human society—labeled universal reformation by the reformers of the early modern period—was maintained under the broader esoteric discipline called pansophy, a term that, as we have seen, is closely related to Rosicrucianism and to Christian theosophy. Antoine Faivre describes pansophy as "a kindred term" to theosophy, "fashionable with Rosicrucians and Paracelsians, first used by the Platonic and Hermetist philosopher Francesco Patrizi."[16] As he goes on to explain:

> This term combines two notions of theosophy, Wisdom by divine illumination and Light from Nature. In 1596, Bartholomäus Scleus opposed particularist or sectarian

15. Gutiérrez, *Theology of Liberation*, 110.
16. Faivre, *Theosophy, Imagination, Tradition*, 9.

theologians with his "*Mystica Theologia Universalis und Pansophia*," which for him was the same as "*Magia coelestis*" or celestial magic. It is more customary to mean by "Pansophy," as it was defined a little later by Jan Amos Comenius, a system of universal knowledge, all things being ordered and classified by God according to analogical relationships. Or, if you prefer, a knowledge of divine things acquired via the concrete world, i.e., the entire universe, in which the "signatures" or hieroglyphics must first be deciphered. In other words, the Book of Nature helps us understand better Holy Scripture and God Himself. This would reserve the term theosophy for the reverse procedure, knowing the universe thanks to our knowledge of God. But, practically speaking, especially from the eighteenth century onward, "theosophy" is generally used to designate the Pansophic progression as well.[17]

The "essential message of the Rosicrucian Manifestos," according to Faivre, is a pansophic vision of universal reformation:

> the union of the light of grace and the light of Nature, the marriage of religion and science—what, Gorceix wrote pertinently, "Will-Erich Peuckert called, a little hastily, *pansophia*" . . . fundamentally, the ideal is still this synthesis of a science in progress and a living religion.[18]

Pansophia thus encompasses both the progression from a knowledge of the "Book of Nature" to the knowledge of God through decoding the "signatures" of the divine in the natural world, as well as the drive to reform all human institutions, including the sciences, religion, the arts, and society, according to this newly acquired universal knowledge. Comenius, with whom the term pansophy is most often associated, provided the clearest explication of these goals in his multi-volume *Consultatio Catholica*, which includes books on the universal reform of education, religion, politics, and language, among other subjects. During his lifetime, only the first volume of the *Consultatio* was published,

17. Ibid., 9–10.
18. Ibid., 84.

INTRODUCTION

the introductory book *Panegersia*, or Universal Awakening.[19] Comenius was thus producing volumes of what twentieth-century theology would label the social gospel many centuries before the reformist awakening of the modern liberal Protestant churches, theological books in which the drive to reform society was directly linked with the Christian quest to understand God and the nature of God's creation.

The notion that nature contains signatures or hieroglyphs of the divine that can be retraced in an ascent to God from nature is an essentially Neoplatonic schema derived from Plotinus and Iamblichus's notion of there being temporal traces of the One in the material cosmos.[20] But Western esoteric sources frequently go beyond a mere embrace of nature understood as the earthly ecological world to include the holistic idea of Nature as the whole integral macrocosm—all of created existence in time and space understood as the manifestation of God, the "Infinite Plenum of All Perfection" according to the grandiose phrase of twentieth-century occultist Frater Achad.[21] This means that the pansophic Book of Nature also includes *history*—both of the cosmos itself and of human beings and human societies. As Sasha Chaitow explains,

> Pansophy is understood as a way of . . . viewing human history through a form of allegorical hermeneutics, whereby events are interpreted as part of a larger narrative in which events within the human microcosm reflect the celestial macrocosm, and can be revealed through myths, legends, and their correspondences.[22]

---

19. A. M. O. Dobbie has provided English translations of all the volumes of the *Consultatio Catholica*, including the introductory volume. See Comenius, *Panergesia or Universal Awakening*.

20. For the Neoplatonic origin of this doctrine, see Shaw, *Theurgy and the Soul*.

21. Frater Achad (Charles Stansfeld Jones) uses some variation of "Infinite Plenum" in many of his late letters, drawing from Universal Brotherhood doctrines, which we will explore further in chapter one.

22. Chaitow, "Making the Invisible Visible," 24.

INTRODUCTION

On this basis, there is a clear possibility of fruitful dialogue between Christian liberation theology and Western esotericism (particularly those branches of it that continue to espouse some version of pansophy), both of which argue that traces of the divine can be found in the upheavals and struggles of human (and cosmic) history, and that a utopian vision of radical social transformation is a necessity for the faithful religious believer.

Shadows of a Future Aeon

Yet the choice of Western esotericism might still seem like an outlandish option for a dialogue with mainstream theology. Some of the occult speculations drawn upon in this study seem to fall into the popular critique often applied to the scholastic theology of the High Middle Ages: weren't the Scholastics more interested in abstract and unsolvable questions like "How many angels can fit on the head of a pin?" than they were in simple evangelical truths and Christian discipleship? In the case of the occultists, perhaps the straw man question with which the figures in this study would be concerned would be something more like, "How many spirits are evoked through the magical chakra-gate of the star Sirius?" Yet the point stands: Isn't most of what I'm referencing here, speculative as it is, a distraction at best, and a deviant and destructive alternative to simple biblical truth at worst? And even if only a distraction, how can any of these people prove this stuff, anyway?

To this critique, I would like to apply the important point that the Thelemic *enfant terrible*, Kenneth Grant, famously made at the end of the introduction to his book, *Outside the Circles of Time*. Grant is often considered one of the strangest and most difficult modern occult writers, but this is perhaps his most lucid moment:

> One final point is here relevant, and I state it without apology. It is not my purpose to try to prove anything; my aim is to construct a magic mirror capable of reflecting

some of the less elusive images seen as shadows of a future aeon.[23]

This eschatological purpose, this attempt to catch a glimpse in the mirror of some "shadows of a future aeon," should be understood to be at the religious heart of many seemingly bizarre, implausible, or downright ridiculous claims made within speculative occultism. Grant goes on to conclude his introduction by stating that, in esoteric writing as in magical practice, it is often by an "architecture of absence" that the real building is revealed—the "reality-structure" of a future aeon, which is the true content of the work, is only made visible through carefully building an "alien structure" with his words and images.[24]

In this sense, occultism emerges from what Catholic theologian Edward Schillebeeckx called "negative contrast experience"—the resolute sense by human beings that our experience of reality, often marked by suffering, injustice, and a lack of meaning, cannot be the whole story.[25] In these moments of lack we feel certain that what we see and experience isn't everything; there must be more meaning to this seemingly cold and empty universe—a *telos*, an end-point, a future transformation. The religious practices, art, culture, and activism that emerges out of these moments attempt to express our sense that there must indeed be meaning and wholeness to our cosmos.

Occultism is one of these practices, regardless of its bizarreries. And, according to Schillebeeckx, what emerges from these practices—diverse as they are, and united only in their unshakeable sense that real human flourishing and meaning might be elusive but *must* be possible, somewhere or somewhen—is not a positive picture of what Schillebeeckx calls the *humanum*, the glorified human being in its eschatological completeness, but in fact is an apophatic image, as in the negative of a photograph, of what the *humanum* will look like at the eschaton. In other words,

---

23. Grant, *Outside the Circles of Time*, 12.
24. Ibid., 12.
25. Schillebeeckx, "Erfahrung und Glaube," 8–9.

a "shadow of a future aeon," revealed through an "architecture of absence," through an "alien structure" haunted by the shape of the real building.

In the end, Kenneth Grant is not too far off from St. Paul here in arguing that the shape of the human and of human society in the last age—as distant to our present imaginings as the farthest star—can only be grasped "through a glass, darkly."[26] What Grant and the other esotericists are willing to do, unlike many mainstream Christian theologians, is to embrace the darkness of the glass.

---

26. 1 Cor 13:12 (KJV).

Creation and Fall

I

The One Idea

The Word that was with God and was God, is the Logos, the Expression of Himself.

This is the Supreme and Integral Word of which all other words are only aspects, reflections, images, anagogues, and metaphors.

God is the One Word which is ever being uttered, and yet, at the same time, which ever remains unuttered. It is uttered by Himself from all Eternity and is the Reason for which all things exist; but because God is transcendentally beyond all names and above the reason of all his creatures, His Word remains unuttered throughout all duration.

—"Word Symbolism," *Shrine of Wisdom*[1]

THE GOSPEL OF JOHN begins famously with its cosmic vision of the universe's creation through the Word: "In the beginning was the Word, and the Word was with God, and the Word was God. He was in the beginning with God. All things came into being through him, and without him not one thing came into being."[2] This opening, which provided the impetus for the advanced Logos theology of the patristic era, also provides the basis for the Christian esoteric vision of a macrocosm founded through a sacred language—in the precincts of Christian and Hermetic Qabalah, usually Hebrew—a kind of prismatic expression in the form of the material universe of the One Word of God, the God-

1. "Word Symbolism," 44.
2. John 1:1–3 (NRSV).

Man Jesus Christ. The *Shrine of Wisdom*, an esoteric journal with a Platonic Christian and comparative religious bent from the first half of the twentieth century, elucidates the Western esoteric Logos theology as the basis for its conception of the cosmos in numerous early issues.[3] In the essay "Word Symbolism," the *Shrine of Wisdom* editors explain how God the Word can both be uttered—immanent in creation as "the Reason for which all things exist"—and unuttered—"transcendentally beyond all names and above the reason of all his creatures."[4]

There is not much here that would be alien to the Christian Platonism of the church fathers. Where the representatives of the Western esoteric tradition begin to expand the scope of the Logos theology outlined here is in their conception of human language's relationship to the Word. The *Shrine of Wisdom* explains that the use of "Word" to describe the Logos is not only a metaphor—in fact, the Logos is "the Supreme and Integral Word of which all other words are only aspects, reflections, images, anagogues, and metaphors."[5] Another source, Frater Recnartus (Heinrich Traenker, a German occultist and pansopher of the Weimar era), explains how the letters of various languages are—as prismatic expressions of the One Word of God—symbols linking heaven and earth, God and humanity:

> The letters of all languages are to be considered as symbols that stand in direct relation to the highest forces and ideas in the universe . . . The letters form a systematic connection between the earthly and the spiritual, the

---

3. *Shrine of Wisdom*. This publication was the journal of the Universal Order, a Christian Hermetic/Platonic society that is still active today in the United Kingdom and offers correspondence courses on esoteric and mystical topics. Its teachings brought together the lesser teachings of the American esoteric order called the Universal Brotherhood—led during the first half of the twentieth century by Frater Achad (Charles Stansfeld Jones), the "magical son" and former protégé of Aleister Crowley—with the Platonism of historical figures like Thomas Taylor.

4. "Word Symbolism," 44.

5. Ibid., 44.

THE ONE IDEA

temporal and the eternal, the changeable and the lasting, the outer and the inner life, between man and God.[6]

This esoteric conception of language allows the occultist to study the "systematic connection" between heaven and the earth represented by the alphabet and thereby to construct a system of correspondences between "the changeable and the lasting, the outer and the inner life, between man and God." The manipulation of these correspondences, drawing on the Hermetic theory of the macrocosm and the microcosm, constitutes the basis of theurgy, or what is called "high magic" in modern occult parlance.[7]

Frater Recnartus goes on to explain the holy alphabet in terms of divine light:

> If we think the letters of a holy alphabet arranged in a circle and receiving light from the center, seven points of the periphery are especially bright, and of these seven, five are brilliant. It is needless to say that we mean the vowels. Since the beginning of time, the vowels, on account of their tattvic and mystic vibrations, have been considered the creators of all objects on the physical plane. The diphthongs are the creators of all things on the astral and mental planes, while the consonants are the creators of the spiritual, divine world. The seven vowels, and especially the five brilliant ones, are portals to the inner world.[8]

Recnartus here transforms the Logos theology of Christian orthodoxy, reframing the Gospel of John's vision of the creation of the universe through the Word into an emanationist account in which all the parts of the cosmos came into being through the vowels. In both cases, the Word or the integral components of the Word are mystic links between the divine world and the created world.

Frater Recnartus also utilizes the prismatic metaphor to describe this process, describing the holy alphabet as points of light

---

6. Recnartus, "Pansophy," 143.
7. See, for example, Cicero and Cicero, *Essential Golden Dawn*.
8. Recnartus, "Pansophy," 144.

on the periphery of the great circle of the cosmos, "receiving light from the center" which is the Godhead. In the tradition of the Hermetic Order of the Golden Dawn, this sacred center is called the Divine White Brilliance, the qabalistic Kether from which the lower sephiroth which make up the Tree of Life emanate:

> Kether is the sphere that contains all that was, is, and will be—it is the place of first emanation and ultimate return. The Crown is the sphere of pure spiritual being; the point of absolute Unity without division—ultimate peace and oneness. Kether is the dwelling place of the Divine White Brilliance, the Godhead . . . It is the Source of All and the Highest Divine Essence of which we can conceive; the Primum Mobile or First Whirlings of Manifestation . . .[9]

In the tradition of the Universal Brotherhood, the cosmos is also described as a great circle—indeed, the name for the Brotherhood itself among its initiates is the *Mahacakra*, Sanskrit for "great circle." As Frater Achad—the third Mahaguru or leader of the Universal Brotherhood—explains in one of his unpublished Universal Brotherhood documents, "The M. [Mahacakra] in its largest sense represents The Great Circle of the Macrocosm with all creatures as its periphery and God Himself as its Centre."[10]

With this teaching of the Universal Brotherhood we return full circle to the *Shrine of Wisdom*'s Johannine conception of the Logos as the One Word "that was with God and was God": the Word as the incarnation of the divine white light, kaleidoscoping—as if through a prism—into a holy alphabet that serves as the earthly expression of the Godhead. In its capacity as the Logos through which the material cosmos was created, the Universal Brotherhood equates the One Word with the One Idea of God—the divine conception or blueprint of the cosmos held in the mind of the great architect. The *Shrine of Wisdom* reiterates this concept, suggesting that all ideas or *logoi* (understood in the archetypal Platonic sense) are "micrologoi" of the "macrologos," the One Idea: "Ideas are Logoi inasmuch as they are aspects of deific words or

---

9. Cicero and Cicero, *Self-Initiation*, 61.
10. Achad writing as Adyton-Alcyon, "Silver Postmesospheric," 1.

archetypes, and every word is a micrologos of the macrologos, that is to say, it is a sign or symbol of an idea, while every real Idea is an aspect of the one idea which is the Logos."[11]

Similarly, in the tradition of the orthodox church fathers, St. Maximus the Confessor explains how everything in the created world has a *logos* that preceded it in the mind of God:

> For we believe that a logos of angels preceded their creation, a logos preceded the creation of each of the beings and powers that fill the upper world, a logos preceded the creation of human beings, a logos preceded everything that receives its becoming from God, and so on . . .[12]

However, according to Dragos Bahrim, "these logoi that precede the beings and the things in the world do not have an existence before actual existence; they are only meditations, thoughts of God."[13] The *logoi* are not substances; rather they are the reasons for substances—they provide the blueprint for created things held in the One Idea of God as the meditations or thoughts of God. Connecting Logos theology to the Wisdom tradition in the Bible—in Proverbs 8, for example, Wisdom is said to have been with God in the beginning, a clear parallel to John 1—the One Idea is also known as the wisdom of God, corresponding in Hermetic Qabalah to the second sephira, Chokmah or Wisdom, the first sphere to emanate from the Divine White Brilliance of Kether.[14]

How does this high theological conception of the One Idea, and its Hermetic expression in terms of magical correspondences, relate to the sociopolitical sphere of everyday human life, and to liberation theology's emphasis on restructuring human society in order to manifest God's kingdom on Earth? In sociological terms, the prismatic manifestation of the One Idea is the ideal social order which is always held as a thought in the mind of God, existing from before time. The prismatic manifestation of the One Idea

11. "Word Symbolism," 45.

12. Maximus the Confessor, *Ambigua* 7, P. G. 91, 1080A, cited in Bahrim, "Anthropic Cosmology of St. Maximus," 14.

13. Ibid., 13.

14. See Fortune, *Mystical Qabalah*, ch. 16.

in the world of human affairs thus becomes the utopian human civilization, a society perfectly founded upon and reflecting God's word. It is our responsibility to pave the way for the manifestation of this ideal society—this social reflection of the One Idea—in the empiric reality of the terrestrial world by our own effort. God will not just activate this ideal within the world with a flick of the divine wrist without human cooperation, without the fulfillment of a human project.

Eliphas Lévi—born Alphonse Louis Constant—the nineteenth-century French magus who is frequently called the founder of modern occultism, began his writing career as a Roman Catholic deacon and a radical socialist, espousing what he called *communisme néo-catholique*.[15] Recent scholarship has shown that Lévi did not abandon his radical political ideas once he concentrated his attention on writing magical and occult tracts in the 1850s; in fact, Lévi saw his occult and qabalistic ideas as the expression of true religion (which he equated with his brand of Neo-Catholicism) and of true socialism.[16] In his preliminary discourse to the second edition of his occult classic, *Dogme et rituel de la haute magie* (usually translated as the *Dogma and Ritual of High Magic* or, by British occultist A.E. Waite, as *Transcendental Magic*), Lévi explains—echoing Logos theology and the occult notions of the Word described above—how the creation of the cosmos is enacted through the "intelligent power which works through universal movement," which he calls "the Verb."[17] The Verb, according to Lévi, is "the initiative of God, which can never remain without effect, and never stops without achieving its goal." The Verb is divine action, and through it God created the cosmos. Lévi explicitly equates the Verb with the Logos in John 1: "In the principle was the Verb, said Saint John the evangelist. In what principle? In the first principle; in the absolute principle

---

15. For a general overview of Eliphas Lévi and his milieu, see McIntosh, *Eliphas Lévi and the French Occult Revival*.

16. See especially the important work of Strube, "Socialist Religion and the Emergence of Occultism."

17. Lévi, *Doctrine and Ritual*, 459.

which comes before all things. Thus, in this principle was the Verb, that is to say, action."[18] In other words, the Word—the One Idea—was held in the Divine White Brilliance of Kether, or the first principle; God's speaking of the Word is equivalent to God's action in creation, which is always ongoing.

Like many occultists, Lévi thus attributes a divine power to speech and to language, and human beings are capable of harnessing this power. According to Lévi, for God,

> speaking is doing; and such should be the power of speech even among men: true speech is the seed of action. An emission of intelligence and will cannot be sterile unless there was abuse or profanation of its original dignity."[19]

Lévi suggests that human speech should result in right action to further God's creation of the world—when it does not, it is because there has been an abuse of the original dignity of the human verb. But in its pristine condition, human action in the world is perfectly aligned with human speech, with truth—and this is a perfect expression of the divine Verb, the One Idea of God.

Lévi, the mystical socialist, suggests that human action in the world and in history, if aligned with the secret truths of the true religion—which is, according to him, Qabalah understood as identical with the universal (catholic) faith—participates in the ongoing creation of the cosmos: "Truth is life, and is revealed through movement. Also through movement, through willed and effective movement, through action, to use a single word, life develops and takes on new forms."[20] In Lévi, the Logos theology of the church fathers and of the occultists becomes the impetus to change history, through his linking of the high magical manipulation of the Hermetic correspondences—made known through the study of the One Idea and its terrestrial manifestation—to an activist spirituality which seeks the transformation of the world:

18. Ibid., 459.
19. Ibid., 460.
20. Ibid., 459.

> The Verb is not an abstraction: it is the most positive principle in the world, because it is continually made evident by deeds. The philosophy of the Verb is essentially the philosophy of action and of done deeds, and it is in this manner that we can distinguish a verb from a word. Words can sometimes be sterile, like a harvest of empty corn husks, but such is never the case with the Verb. The Verb, is the full and fertile word; men do not amuse themselves by listening to and applauding it; they always fulfill it![21]

Later on, Lévi calls the Hermetic study of universal natural forces—his qabalistic understanding of mathematics and the magical correspondences to which it gives rise—the "supreme and inevitable consequence of the works of the human spirit, this conquest of divinity by intelligence and by study," which must "complete the redemption of the human soul and provide the definitive emancipation of the Verb of humanity."[22] Doing so will finally cause what we call natural law to correspond to revealed law, science to religion. From this "reconciliation of the human Verb shall be born true morality," which Lévi connects to the history of the European revolutionary period:

> The immortality of the human Verb proven through terrible convulsions, by a frenzied revolt, by gigantic battles and by suffering similar to that of Prometheus, until the arrival of a man strong enough to reconnect humanity to God: that is the history of the entire revolution![23]

Lévi's specific historical examples might be dated by modern standards, or even historically questionable (he launches into an extended mystical paean to Peter the Great), but his overall point here is clear. The human verb, aligned with the divine Verb or the Word of God, can and must remake the world through action in history. Lévi concludes his discourse with a stirring

---

21. Ibid., 460.
22. Ibid., 462.
23. Ibid., 469.

description of how a people could become the liberating people of God, the verb of humanity:

> After the reform and the revolution in Napoleon's wake had shaken the base of all of Europe's powers, after the negation of the divine right had transformed almost all of the masters of world into usurpers and handed over the political universe to atheism or the fetishism of the parties, one sole people, guardians of the doctrines of unity and authority, had become the people of God in politics. And that people grew in strength in an impressive manner, inspired by an idea that could be transformed into a Verb, that is to say into a word of action . . .[24]

According to Lévi, to embody the Verb in this manner, to become the "people of God in politics" that will transform human society into the social manifestation of the One Idea, human beings must first understand the Hermetic correspondences between the microcosm and the macrocosm, the expressions of the Word in the form of the "divine alphabet" that underlies all terrestrial phenomena, including social phenomena. In the next chapter, we will turn to the Hermetic Qabalah and its system of correspondences, but through the lens of the One Idea for human society—the hierarchy of forces behind the ideal society held in the mind of God, and the fallen society we experience throughout our everyday lives in the world as it is.

---

24. Ibid., 469.

II

Social Qabalah

> The Secret Tradition contains, firstly, the memorials of a loss which has befallen humanity; and, secondly, the records of a restitution in respect of that which was lost. For reasons which I do not propose to consider at the present stage, the keepers of the tradition perpetuated it in secret by means of the Instituted Mysteries and cryptic literature.
>
> —A. E. Waite[1]

IN THE PREVIOUS CHAPTER, we examined the doctrine of the Logos, the Word of God or the One Idea, from the perspective of a number of Western esoteric traditions. Through this One Idea of God the whole created world emerged, as recounted biblically in the first chapter of the Gospel of John. The sociopolitical expression or prismatic manifestation of the One Idea is the ideal social order—a civilization founded upon and perfectly reflecting God's will for creation. But what is God's will for creation, and why isn't it already in place?

In the Bible, Paul of Tarsus calls Satan the "god of this world," and the Letter to the Ephesians states that "our struggle is not against enemies of blood and flesh, but against the rulers, against the authorities, against the cosmic powers of this present darkness, against the spiritual forces of evil in the heavenly places."[2] The biblical witness thus suggests that we live in a fallen cosmos ruled by cosmic powers of evil. Walter Wink, the writer of a classic

---

1. Waite, *Secret Tradition in Freemasonry*, ix.
2. 2 Cor 4:4 and Eph 6:12 (NRSV).

theological trilogy on the powers, utilized these biblical notions to construct "a cosmology of power in which 'spirituality' is seen . . . as being the 'interiority'—or 'angel'—of people, institutions and even nations."[3] In this present darkness, the "interiorities" or "angels" of people, institutions, and nations are fallen, and thus corrupted from their true reasons for being which are held in the One Idea of God.

Wink's theology of the powers could not have been written without the prior work of Episcopal lay theologian William Stringfellow, perhaps the foremost demonologist of the modern era. Stringfellow locates the fallen powers and principalities at work in the images, institutions, and ideologies to which humanity pays homage, serving these idols in the mistaken belief that doing so will bring us meaning and freedom from our finite human existences. But according to Stringfellow, we are mistaken to give them our allegiance—because we live in the era called the fall, all the powers and principalities of this world (and all human beings) are fallen creatures. And Stringfellow is clear throughout his works that the ultimate end of all the fallen principalities and powers, of all images, institutions, and ideologies, is nothing other than death:

> Death is greater than any of the principalities and powers, and none of them prevail against it. The whole of creation exists under the reign of death. Men die. Images, though they survive us for a time, also die. Institutions and ideologies, though they have immense survival capabilities, eventually die. Nations die. The reality which survives them all is death itself. Death, it seems, is the decisive, ultimate and dominant truth in history. No man is safe from his own death who looks for his salvation in idolatry of some principality, whatever it may be.[4]

All the fallen powers and principalities of this present darkness ultimately serve "the god of this world," which Stringfellow identifies as death itself. Stringfellow's analysis of social evils, of

3. McIntosh, "Engaging Walter Wink's Powers," 102–3.
4. Stringfellow, *Free in Obedience*, 64.

the domination system of the powers in our corrupt and unjust society—what the Rev. Dr. Martin Luther King Jr. called the "giant triplets" of racism, militarism, and economic inequality—is ultimately a biblical theology that lucidly describes how the fallen creation is at war with itself and with humanity in the form of the powers and principalities, who ultimately serve death as their only lord.

Yet, as Stringfellow proclaimed in Baltimore in 1968 at a church gathering during the trial of the Catonsville Nine, imprisoned for burning draft cards during the Vietnam War, "The grace of Jesus Christ in this life is that death fails."[5] All is not hopeless: Stringfellow, as a Christian theologian, sees Jesus Christ—the incarnate Word of God, the power of the resurrection—as the answer to the fallen principalities, as the victory that defeats death here and now:

> [Christ's] power over death is effective, not just at the terminal point of a man's life, but throughout his life, during this life in this world, right now. This power is effective in the times and places in the daily lives of individuals when they are so gravely and relentlessly assailed by the claims of principalities for an idolatry which, in spite of all its disguises, really surrenders to death as the reigning presence in the world. His resurrection means the possibility of living in this life, in the very midst of death's works, safe and free from death.[6]

Because of the cosmic power of Christ's resurrection, Stringfellow suggests, we can live in the world knowing that death does not have the last word—as Paul says, "O death, where is thy sting? O grave, where is thy victory?"[7] Stringfellow's constant proclamation of the militant power of the Word of God—the One Idea incarnate in Jesus Christ—in the midst of the fall, a power that renews creation and sets it aright in the eschatological peaceable kingdom, offers a positive vision of the *telos* of history—and of the

---

5. Dear, "The World—and Word," para. 11.
6. Stringfellow, *Free in Obedience*, 72.
7. 1 Cor 15:55 (KJV).

powers and principalities themselves—even as he gives us a dire image of our present-day reality.

Stringfellow thus has a positive side when it comes to the powers and principalities. The powers and principalities are, according to Stringfellow, fellow creatures, declared good by God during the creation of the world (Gen 1:31), and they will ultimately be—and, in some sense, have already been—reconciled to God and each other in Christ Jesus. The powers of this world will not be obliterated or destroyed—they will be redeemed in Christ, just as fallen humanity is redeemed. As Stringfellow explains in *Free in Obedience:*

> Christ's resurrection is for men and for the whole of creation, including the principalities of this world. Through the encounters between Christ and death, the power of death is exhausted. The reign of death and, within that, the pretensions to sovereignty over history of the principalities, is brought to an end in Christ's resurrection.[8]

The primary source for cosmogonic theology in the Western esoteric tradition, and for meditations on the powers and principalities, their fall and their redemption, is the Hermetic Qabalah.[9] Like Stringfellow and Walter Wink, but in an esoteric and occult key, this tradition sees categorizing, understanding, and working with the cosmic powers as a necessary task for the qabalist, who traditionally aims for both his or her personal mystical union with the divine and for the reconciliation of all things in God. In that sense, though coming from a very different historical and religious context from Stringfellow, the Hermetic Qabalah agrees with Stringfellow that the powers and principalities of this world, though currently fallen, are destined for reconciliation with God.

For the Christian cabalists of the Renaissance, who greatly influenced the development of Hermetic Qabalah, Stringfellow's admonition to Christians to confront "the noise and verbiage and

---

8. Stringfellow, *Free in Obedience*, 73.

9. "Qabalah" is the spelling traditionally used to refer to the Western esoteric and Hermetic Qabalah, as distinguished from traditional Jewish mystical Kabbalah and Christian Renaissance Cabala.

falsehood of death with the truth and potency and efficacy of the Word of God," to "know the Word, teach the Word, nurture the Word, preach the Word, define the Word, incarnate the Word, do the Word, live the Word," would not at all be alien to their work in defining the qabalistic name of Jesus—"Yeheshuah" in the Western esoteric tradition, including in the Hermetic Order of the Golden Dawn—as the key to the qabalistic mysteries, as the Word that can set all the cosmic powers of the world back into their proper relationship to each other, to humanity, and to the One Idea of God.[10]

Ever since the Renaissance synthesis of Christian theology with Neoplatonic theurgy, Jewish Kabbalistic mysticism, and the medieval traditions of alchemy, grimoire magic, and Islamic astrology, Christian esotericists have also seen their mission in terms of exposing "death and all death's works and wiles," casting out demons, performing exorcisms, cleansing the possessed, and raising "those who are dead in mind and conscience," as Stringfellow further defines the vocation of a Christian.[11] Indeed, as the first Rosicrucian manifesto—the "*Fama Fraternitatis*"—states, the Rosicrucian adepts—those heirs to the Renaissance magi and to the traditions of Christian Cabala—are to live among the nations following "the custom of the country," healing, performing exorcisms, and teaching like the early disciples of Jesus: "none of them should profess any other thing, then to cure the sick, and that gratis."[12]

In terms of the powers and principalities, the Western esoteric tradition has always recognized both the dangers of the cosmic powers and the responsibility of the qabalist toward them. As Peregrin Wildoak, a prominent commentator on the spirituality of the Hermetic Order of the Golden Dawn, states,

> [H]umanity is made in the image of the One. That is, we have been created to be the self-reflective and self-cognizant aspect of the world (at least at this stage of the world's unfoldment). We are to be the facilitators of a current of blessing stemming from the Unmanifest One

---

10. Stringfellow, *William Stringfellow*, 169.
11. Ibid., 169.
12. "Fama Fraternitatis," 105.

and directed to the Manifest All. By being conscious and allowing God to move through us, God is transferred to all we behold and touch and engage with . . . When we move into the elemental realms and engage with elemental Beings we help form a circuit between the Unmanifest One and the elemental Beings and kingdoms. While we are the bridge that allows this to occur, we cannot consider ourselves as better or more important than either of the two other aspects of this circuit; the Unmanifest or the elemental Beings. A wire is no more important than the two ends of the electric circuit it connects, as all three points are needed for electricity to flow. This is what true alliance is about—the realization that we are required to work in partnership and harmony with other Beings for the mutual unfoldment of all.[13]

According to Wildoak, the task of the Hermetic qabalist is to see "ourselves as but one interconnected aspect of the great unfolding of the manifest universe," which is the proper "view of the initiate" of the Hermetic mysteries. There are echoes here of Dr. King's stirring view of the "interrelated structure of reality," as, for example, when he suggests in "Letter from a Birmingham Jail" that we are "caught an inescapable network of mutuality, tied in a single garment of destiny."[14]

In fact, the Hermetic or qabalistic perspective is not very different from the Neoplatonic Christian theology of church fathers like Maximus, who expanded on Pseudo-Dionysius the Areopagite to explain how the human being, as the microcosm, was responsible for acting as the mediator who would bring all of the cosmos—the macrocosm—back into reconciliation with God, the One, in Jesus Christ.[15] Though the mystical practices involved and some of the phraseology might seem exotic or even disreputable—the free use of theurgic magic, the Tarot symbols, and the veneration or honoring of pagan god-forms—the long tradition of

---

13. Wildoak, *By Names and Images*, 241.
14. King, "Letter from a Birmingham Jail," para. 4.
15. See, for example, Thunberg, *Microcosm and Mediator*.

Hermetic Qabalah has much in common with the Christian Neoplatonism of Maximus and Pseudo-Dionysius.

In what follows, using the broad outline of the Hermetic Qabalah—specifically, that nearly ubiquitous glyph called the Tree of Life and its ten spheres, the sephiroth—we will examine what the ideal social order looks like in its pristine emanation, as well as what society looks like in this era called the fall, drawing both from Western esoteric sources and from radical Christian theologians like Stringfellow and Wink. And we will also consider the path of return—the social and mystical process necessary to reintegrate the cosmos with the One Idea, to rejoin the microcosm with the macrocosm, and thereby to draw all things into union with God.

I. Kether—Divine White Brilliance

The first *sephirah*, or sphere, of Kether, known in the Hermetic Order of the Golden Dawn as the Divine White Brilliance, is, as Chic and Sandra Cicero explain, "the sphere that contains all that was, is, and will be—it is the place of first emanation and ultimate return . . . Kether is the dwelling place of the Divine White Brilliance, the Godhead."[16] As the sphere of the first whirlings of creation or the *Primum Mobile*, the Prime Mover, Kether is the originary point from which the rest of creation emanates, the still small point which contains in concentration all that is and will be. In the eschaton, all things will return to Kether in their union with the Godhead. Many occult techniques, including the "Magic of Light" of the Golden Dawn, attempt to draw down the divine light from Kether to realign or reintegrate the rest of the Tree of Life—and thus, the cosmos—with the light of God, with the divine will and intention for the universe.

---

16. Cicero and Cicero, *Self-Initiation*, 61.

II. Chokmah—The One Idea

Corresponding in the Hermetic Qabalah to the second sphere or sephira of Chokmah, the One Idea, as explicated in our previous chapter, is the wisdom or Logos of God through which all the diversity of creation emerges as if light through a prism. In Chokmah, the Divine White Light of Kether kaleidoscopes into the many colors of the cosmos—the lower spheres of the Tree of Life. In terms of the sociopolitical realm, the One Idea provides the concentrated ideal of society—the perfect goodness, truth, and beauty that is expressed in social terms as just institutions, equality under the law, peace between and within nations, and economic equality.

In Christian terms, Chokmah is the sphere of Christ as the Logos or Word of God, through whom "all things came into being" (John 1:2). Sociologically speaking, Jesus Christ provides the model for a just society, for creation in its ideal form. Edward Schillebeeckx provocatively writes that "christology is *concentrated* creation: belief in creation as God wills it to be."[17] Christology for Schillebeeckx is "not a new divine plan for a creation which has gone wrong," rather "it is the supreme expression of God's eternally new being which we can perceive to some degree only from ongoing creation and its history."[18] Christology is thus the expression of our understanding of God's One Idea for creation in a concentrated way, in Jesus Christ who mediates God for Christians amidst the contingency of human history, including human societies and institutions. The theological explication of who Jesus Christ is—Christology—is for Christians the perfect expression of what the living God wills creation to be. Thus Chokmah, or the One Idea, is itself "concentrated creation," the cosmos in a condensed or epitomized form.

---

17. Schillebeeckx, *Interim Report on the Books*, 128.
18. Ibid., 128.

III. Binah—Immaculate Conception

The third *sephira*, Binah, is traditionally translated as "Understanding." Binah, in its location on the pillar of severity, is the harshly binding and constricting force that begins to give shape and definition to creation. Here the line linking Kether with Chokmah becomes a triangle, the supernal triad of the three *sephiroth* described by Israel Regardie as the "dynamic life and root of all things," which dwell above the Abyss that separates the Godhead from the lower realm of manifestation.[19] God is identified here as the Holy Spirit in the world, the Spirit which broods over the formless, oceanic darkness of the Abyss—the sophianic mirror of creation. This is a pneumatological vision of creation which posits the Holy Spirit as God's active presence "in and with the contingent," the divinity undergirding the manifest world, the divine Sophia.[20] In Schillebeeckx's later writings, the Spirit and the grace ever present in creation—present from the ground up due to God's "good act of creation"—are almost identified as one and the same.[21] According to Schillebeeckx, grace and nature are not completely dualistic, or at odds with each other—though creation is not God and God is God, creation is necessarily always within the presence of the living God.[22]

Binah is, to use the phrase given by St. Maximillian of Kolbe to describe the Holy Spirit, the "uncreated Immaculate Conception"—the Spirit of God which impregnates the cosmos from before its creation, the force which results in a miraculous emanation from nothing, grace immaculately constructing the universe from the ground up.[23] Maximillian gave the Holy Spirit this title because he saw an intimate connection between the Spirit

---

19. Regardie, introduction to *The Golden Dawn*, cited by Cicero and Cicero, *Essential Golden Dawn*, xiii.

20. Schillebeeckx, *God Among Us*, 94. For a Catholic interpretation of Sophiology, which has much in common with the theology outlined here, see Cselényi, *Maternal Face of God?*

21. Schillebeeckx, *Understanding of Faith*, 98.

22. Schillebeeckx, *Interim Report*, 114.

23. Maximillian, *Kolbe Reader*, 211–12.

and the Virgin Mary as the "created" Immaculate Conception, going so far as to describe Mary as a "quasi-incarnation" of the Holy Spirit. For Maximillian, the Virgin Mary is the exemplar of divinization, of the Holy Spirit overshadowing the creature and rendering it quasi-divine—a new concentration of the One Idea whose way is made possible by the Incarnation of the Word, the Spirit-impregnated universe which gives birth to the Cosmic Christ, Mariology as an epitome of Christology. Sociologically speaking, Binah is the human world undergirded by the Spirit of God, the divine justice of the ideal social order emerging in and through the contingent structures of this world.

Daath—City of the Silver Star

Aleister Crowley, for all his anti-Christian rhetoric, himself suggests the connection between the Virgin Mary, the Holy Spirit, and the prospect of a divinized human world. In "On the Powers of Number," Crowley writes:

> The Virgin Mary, herself immaculate, formulates the Christ (in his aspect as Adam Qadmon the Universe undefiled) by the influx of the Divine Spirit or breath. By the Virgin do our prayers ascend unto the Throne . . . Now this card [The High Priestess in the Tarot, representing Mary] is the occult link between the human life and the Divine Light. The High Priestess is the Higher Soul of Man and his aspiration unto the divine. The denial of the Virgin is therefore no less than the unpardonable sin: for it is the denial of the Holy Spirit in oneself.[24]

Much can be said about Crowley's teaching in this paragraph.[25] For now it suffices to say that the One Idea—whose high priestess is the immaculate Virgin Mary—finds incarnation as the Christ by the influx of the Holy Spirit, the descent of the divine light into the material world of "human life," including the

---

24. Crowley, "On the Powers of Number," 4.

25. We will examine it, and its explication of The High Priestess card in the Tarot, further in chapter 4, "The Silver Star of Bethlehem."

structures of human society—the birth of the ideal social order as the conception of the One Idea of God (Chokmah) by the Spirit-infused cosmos (Binah).

The High Priestess in the Tarot, which Crowley attributes here to the Virgin Mary as the quasi-incarnation of the Holy Spirit, is assigned in the Western esoteric tradition to the path between Tiphareth (the fifth sephira, described below) and Kether. This card is also known as the Priestess of the Silver Star, the Silver Star being the symbol used by the Golden Dawn and by Crowley to refer to the order of initiation that lies above the Abyss—the third order that, in the traditional Golden Dawn system, is inaccessible for the individual initiate in this lifetime.[26]

For the individual qabalist, the quasi-sephira of Daath—"Knowledge" in Hebrew—arises from the process of evolution and the balance within the psyche of the two pillars on either side of the Tree of Life. Regardie explains that, as the initiate evolved through magical practice,

> that is to say as he developed sufficient control over his emotions as to be able to remain poised in a detachment from the dual pull of the opposites, so there developed within him a new faculty of discrimination and spiritual discernment.[27]

In Regardie's psychological interpretation of the Golden Dawn system, Daath is conceived to be "a symbolic link, self-induced and self-devised, between the higher genius on the one hand and on the other, the ego, the conscious self."[28]

Translated from the microcosm of human psychology to the mesocosm of human society, Daath is the eschatological City of the Silver Star, the link between the divine intention and the conscious aspirations of human civilization. It is the ideal society which is born through the willed conjunction of the One Idea

---

26. Cicero and Cicero, *Essential Golden Dawn*, 143. Crowley, of course, would assert the possibility of attaining these third order grades within his A∴A∴ system, which he designed to surpass and supersede the Golden Dawn.

27. Regardie, *Middle Pillar*, 70.

28. Ibid., 74.

with the Spirit brooding over the blank tablet of creation, Chokmah with Binah. It is the accomplishment of the human project, what Martin Luther King Jr. called the world house or the beloved community.[29] This city is always already emerging through the advent of the Spirit, but will not be built in its fullness until the end of time. It is the kingdom of God on earth, the raising of the earthly city into the heavenly city—the dwelling place of the hidden or inner church. We will explore these concepts further in the chapters which follow.

IV. Chesed—The Universal Church

Now that we are below the Abyss and the supernal triad, we can examine the remaining sephiroth in terms of fully human concepts and institutions. In the social Qabalah, the fourth sephira, Chesed—"mercy" in Hebrew—corresponds to religion as a universal human phenomenon, and in the ideal social order to the universal church which encompasses all human religious institutions that manifest the truth of the One Idea. This church heralds the progressive in-breaking of the City of the Silver Star. Chesed as the universal church is not the same concept as the inner church, for it is an exoteric institution rather than an invisible assembly. This is why, in the world as it is now, the fallen world, the universal church is currently a fragmented collection of compromised institutions and religious expressions.

Eliphas Lévi postulated that the union between science and religion which he called high magic—a universal religion—would result in the progressive initiation of humanity, leading ultimately to human emancipation, liberation, and the emergence of the ideal social order.[30] For Lévi, this true religion could be discovered through the study of Qabalah, which would reveal it to be none other than true Catholicism—the purified Catholic

---

29. See King, *Where Do We Go?*

30. This thesis is scattered throughout all of Lévi's occultist works, but see Strube, "Socialist Religion and the Emergence," 378, for a concise summary of Lévi's magical socialism.

Church as the universal church (catholic of course meaning universal), espousing the universal religion that was Lévi's conception of occultism. As Lévi wrote in *The Book of Splendors* about this religion of the future,

> When all religions are dead, the unique and universal religion will live on. This will occur when there is one accord among all men in their belief in universal solidarity, unity of aspiration, diversity of expression, faith in a single God, freedom for symbolism and tolerance of images, orthodoxy in charity, with universality always at the heart of all . . .[31]

As the representation of the mercy of God, Chesed is responsible for balancing the severity of Geburah—the mercy of the universal church versus the strict adherence to the law of the justice system. The ideal church or universal religion would be, in the words of Pope Francis, "open wide to welcome" everyone, no matter their "social status, language, race, culture, religion"— a true vision of catholicity or universality.[32] There is an intimate relationship between mercy and freedom, between welcome and inclusion, which Francis sees in the gospel message: "The Gospel calls us to recognize in the history of humanity the design of a great work of inclusion, which fully respects the freedom of every person, every community, every people."[33] This vision of the church of mercy has much in common with Lévi's prescription for the religion of the future. It is the universal church's job to pave the way for and ensure this freedom, this liberty of the gospel, which includes everyone within its merciful embrace.

---

31. Lévi, *Book of Splendors*, 121. The requirement of "faith in a single God" might seem to contradict the rest of this passage's emphasis on "diversity of expression" and "freedom for symbolism," but Lévi writes this in the context of an esoteric interpretation of Freemasonry. One should thus interpret this as referring to the masonic notion of God—God as the Supreme Being (or perhaps even the Tillichian notion of Ultimate Concern), diversely understood in many different systems, under many different forms of symbolism.

32. "Pope Francis," para. 15.

33. Ibid., para. 2.

V. Geburah—The Justice System

Geburah is the flipside of Chesed—"severity" to Chesed's mercy. Geburah is the justice system—the law in its unyielding harshness. In our fallen world, the justice system is deeply flawed. For example, in the United States today, systemic racism and white supremacy have led to young black males being "nine times more likely to be killed by police officers than other Americans," with the shooters rarely being convicted.[34] The so-called war on drugs provides another example: though "African Americans represent just 12.5 percent of illicit drug users, they make up nearly 30 percent of those arrested for drug offenses."[35] Meanwhile, "tough on crimes" policing "has led to skyrocketing federal discretionary spending on prisons—$7.5 billion in 2017, a tenfold increase over 1976—and increased policing of poor communities to fill them."[36]

These are only examples from the modern-day United States. Throughout history, legal systems have been used to enforce unjust social hierarchies and structural inequalities, from chattel slavery to colonialism. The justice system is frequently anything but just. Yet perhaps surprisingly, justice itself remains a key word of those struggling against oppression all over the world. The ideal of true justice transcends the fallen state of our flawed or corrupt justice systems. In the ideal social order, the justice system's unyielding nature is balanced by Chesed's mercy, and made fair by equality under the law. This is represented allegorically by the image of the blindfolded Lady Justice with her scales, an image that appears in the Tarot card Justice and corresponds to the Egyptian godform Maat. Frater Achad, the wayward protégé of Aleister Crowley, foresaw a coming Aeon of Maat in which the warlike "force and fire" of Crowley's Aeon of Horus would give way to a peaceable Aeon of truth and justice.[37]

---

34. Poor People's Campaign, *Souls of Poor Folk*, 4.

35. Ibid., 4.

36. Ibid., 4.

37. Grant, *Magical Revival*, 161–62. For more on Achad's eschatological vision of the Aeon of Maat, see chapter 6, "City of the Silver Star."

Eschatological justice, then, is what the ideal justice system would enforce—justice that is perfectly fulfilled but is also perfectly tempered by mercy and love. Lévi continually suggests that the "great axiom of occult philosophy" is that "harmony results from the analogy of opposites"—balance is the occult key to realizing the ideal social order.[38] In terms of the qabalistic balance required between Geburah and Chesed, if the Tree of Life is to be experienced in its pristine or reintegrated state, one should heed the words of Dr. King:

> What is needed is a realization that power without love is reckless and abusive, and love without power is sentimental and anemic. Power at its best is love implementing the demands of justice, and justice at its best is power correcting everything that stands against love.[39]

VI. Tiphareth—Commonweal

Tiphareth, the sphere of the sun, is often attributed to the heart center when the Tree of Life is mapped onto a human body, and to messiah figures like Jesus Christ, Osiris, and the Thelemic Horus. Tiphareth is the balanced point in the center of the Tree of Life—if the "great axiom of occult philosophy" is that "harmony results from the analogy of opposites,"[40] then Tiphareth is where that analogy of opposites occurs. Dion Fortune writes that Tiphareth is the "centre of equilibrium of the whole tree, being in the middle of the Central Pillar."[41] In the occult system of the Golden Dawn, the grade attributed to Tiphareth—Adeptus Minor—is the first grade of the second order, the *Rosae Rubeae et Aureae Crucis* or the order of the Ruby Rose and Golden Cross. This is the Rosicrucian grade in which the initiate achieves first contact with her higher self, her Christ consciousness.

38. Lévi, *Book of Splendors*, 96.
39. King, "Where Do We Go?," 247.
40. Lévi, *Book of Splendors*, 96.
41. Fortune, *Mystical Qabalah*, 175.

Christ imagery abounds in Tiphareth. Fortune explains that, from "the point of view of Kether [Tiphareth] is a child; from the point of view of Malkuth it is a king; and from the point of view of the transmutation of force it is a sacrificed god."[42] Tiphareth is the sphere of the Son of God, the Redeemer—the Christ child who is the reflection of Kether in physical manifestation, the Lord to whom all things in Malkuth or the manifest world must pay homage, and the crucified one whose sacrifice restores harmony to the cosmos.

As Fortune continues, in "Tiphareth God is made manifest in form and dwells among us; i.e. comes within range of human consciousness. Tiphareth, the Son, 'shows us' Kether, the Father." The supernal triad of Kether, Chokmah, and Binah is "for ever striving to bring the Kingdom of the six central Sephiroth"—called Adam Kadmon, the archetypal man or *humanum*—

> into a state of equilibrium ... The Redeemer, then, manifests in Tiphareth, and is for ever striving to redeem His Kingdom by re-uniting it to the Supernal across the gulf made by the fall, which separated the lower Sephiroth from the higher, and by bringing the diverse forces of the sixfold kingdom into equilibrium.[43]

In this qabalistic redemption myth, the Daughter (Malkuth) is married to the Son (Tiphareth) and thereby arouses the force of the Father (Chokmah), raising the Daughter to the Throne of the Mother (Binah). Tiphareth is thus the Christic bridegroom who marries the daughter-bride, the church or the cosmos, bringing it into the divinity of the supernals.

The elements of the interpretation of Tiphareth for our social Qabalah are already present in the traditional esoteric sources, with their emphasis on Tiphareth as the Redeemer who forever strives "to redeem His Kingdom by re-uniting it to the Supernal." As the heart center of the Tree of Life, the place of the Cosmic Christ, Tiphareth is the sphere wherein the different parts of the social order

---

42. Ibid., 176.
43. Ibid., 177.

find their balance and harmony—the location of the commonweal or the common good of all people and all parts of society, the *res publica*. Tiphareth is the higher self of a society, a society founded on Jesus' Golden Rule of loving one's neighbor as oneself. Like the initiate of the Golden Dawn, who seeks the knowledge and conversation of his or her higher self in Tiphareth, a society rooted in social justice must be married to Tiphareth, the commonweal, if it is to manifest God's intention for it in the One Idea.

This is the role of Tiphareth-commonweal in the abstract—but in practice, as we well know, all historical human societies have failed to truly marry themselves to Tiphareth. If a society does not root itself in Tiphareth, it is out of balance and reflects the fall rather than the One Idea of God, and this is our historical reality as human beings living in the era called the fall. We need the assistance of Christ the Redeemer to repair this fall and to bring the earthly city back into union with the heart of the cosmos, the commonweal that God intends for God's creation.

Liberation theologians like James Cone, the founder of black liberation theology, identify Jesus Christ as a liberator, as the source of hope for the marginalized and dispossessed in the world today. To seek this Christ—attributed to the sphere of Tiphareth—is to seek not only one's individual salvation or private illumination, but to seek the commonweal, to seek the reintegration of human society with the One Idea of the Creator.

Invoking James Cone is important here, because if the incarnation of Christ in the material world is one aspect of Tiphareth, Cone's theology explains how the incarnation means that the *particular* history of a marginalized Jew living in Roman-occupied Palestine—Jesus of Nazareth—is in fact the mustard seed of the eschatologically rectified cosmic order. Translating this to his mid-twentieth-century context in the United States, Cone uses as his starting point the necessarily *particular* experience of the African American community, a marginalized people whose struggle for freedom provides Cone's theological context. The grounds for starting from the particular rather than the universal in liberation theology is Jesus Christ, for "Christian theology is language about the *liberating* character of God's presence in Jesus Christ as he calls his people into being for freedom in the world."[44] Since this is a liberation that must be seen in the concrete struggles of specific historical groups, liberation theology's language must reflect particular contexts, and must start from the experience of the oppressed rather than the experience of the oppressor.

This can be well illustrated by Cone's critique of influential Protestant theologian Karl Barth's notion that "God's word is alien to humanity and thus comes to it as a 'bolt from the blue'"—this is a true analysis when speaking of the oppressor, the white theologian, but not true from the perspective of the black theologian and black people, as the incarnation shows us that "God's revelation comes . . . in and through the cultural situation of the oppressed."[45] And since, in true Barthian fashion, God's revelation is for Cone an encounter with Jesus Christ, the experience of Christ must necessarily be found "on the ground," in the sweat and struggle of a historically specific oppressed people. Thus, although Cone does not often make specific reference to the traditional theology of the incarnation, I would argue that his Christology is deeply incarnational—Jesus Christ is God's presence in the world, both as a historical, oppressed Jew in first-century Palestine, and as a real ontological reality among the particular struggles of oppressed people today.

Translated to the social Qabalah, this liberationist interpretation of Tiphareth as the Son of God, the Redeemer, means that in a fallen society redemption must come from the marginalized, from the struggles of the poor and dispossessed of our day, for it is there that we can locate the mystical heart center of the redeemed cosmic order. Tiphareth is not attained in abstraction; as the place where "God is made manifest in form and dwells among us," we must discover Tiphareth in the *particular* rather than the universal. We will not find the commonweal of our social Qabalah in abstract speculation about social reform or the proper order of society, still less will we find it in the ideologies of those in power; instead, we

---

44. Cone, *God of the Oppressed*, 8.
45. Cone, *Black Theology of Liberation*, 28.

will find it "on the ground," in and through the "cultural situation of the oppressed."[46] From this liberationist way of the heart, we will discover the Tiphareth center which must be married to the earthly city of Malkuth in order to redeem and repair our society, to reunite it with the One Idea of Chokmah in the supernal triad—a cosmic reintegration which is also a social liberation.

VII. Netzach—The Marketplace

To ascribe the sphere of Netzach to the marketplace or the economic order in our social Qabalah might at first seem odd. Netzach is usually labeled the sphere of Venus—corresponding, in the Hermetic qabalist's charts, to deities of love and fertility. The cosmic processes represented by Netzach cannot be separated from the role of the next sephira, Hod, nor from Yesod, which completes their triangle and equilibrates their energies. Netzach, Dion Fortune explains, contains the undifferentiated and unindividuated energies of the cosmos, powers, and principalities that have not yet been given personal identity or form:

> In Netzach force is still relatively free-moving, being bound only into exceedingly fluidic and ever-shifting shapes, and in Hod taking on for the first time definite and permanent form, though of an exceedingly tenuous nature. In Netzach a particular form of force represents itself as a type of being, flowing backwards and forwards over the boundaries of manifestation in an exceedingly elusive manner. Such beings have no individualised personalities, but are like the armies with banners that can be seen in the sunset clouds. In Hod, however, individualisation into units has taken place, and there is continuity of existence.[47]

The energies in Netzach, then, corresponding to human emotions in microcosmic terms, require the intellect of Hod to refine them into differentiated beings rather than inchoate cosmic

---

46. Cone, *Black Theology of Liberation*, 28.
47. Fortune, *Mystical Qabalah*, 207.

powers—and, in turn, require the astral substance of Yesod to develop them into personal forms.

Netzach is the marketplace in our social Qabalah because, although the mythology of capitalism might suggest otherwise, the economic order is in fact an abstract, impersonal zone, in which commodities are alienated from their true-use value and the labor required to produce them. The marketplace is not a rational zero-sum game; in fact, it is a highly emotional realm in which inequalities tend to abound and innovations rise and fall on the basis of a combination of randomness and market fluctuations. The marketplace is not rational, and it is not alone the producer of popular culture, but all three of those areas of society—economics, the rationally ordered civic bureaucracy, and popular culture—are intertwined and rely on each other to form a coherent triangle.

Without the intellect of Hod, the civic bureaucracy—without, in other words, rational regulations, planning, and regard for the general welfare—the sphere of Netzach, the marketplace, is just a chaotic realm of rising and falling commodities and competing interests. Without Yesod, popular culture, the economic order is a purely abstract realm that lacks form. Just think of the constant need for advertising to create viable products in our late capitalist world, as if they would cease to exist without the status granted to them by the trappings of culture. Most significantly, without being ruled by the higher sephira of Tiphareth, the commonweal, the marketplace of Netzach lacks any moral center, ignoring the concrete needs of the people in favor of oligarchy and corporate greed. Our present immoral economic order, with its massively rising inequality and poverty in the midst of abundance, can amply testify to this.

VIII. Hod—Civic Bureaucracy

Hod cannot be understood apart from Netzach—it is the intellectual sphere, the sphere of Mercury, which concentrates the inchoate powers of Netzach into differentiated ideas or concepts. These powers still lack being—for that, they require the astral substance of Yesod—but have moved closer to taking on individualized identities. Dion Fortune explains:

> Hod is especially the Sphere of Magic, because it is the sphere of the formulation of forms, and is therefore the sphere in which the magician actually works, for it is his mind that formulates the forms, and his will that makes the link with the natural forces of the Sphere of Netzach that ensoul them . . . The meaning of the Hebrew word Hod is Glory, and this suggests at once to the mind that in this, the first Sphere in which forms are definitely organised, the radiance of the Primordial is shown forth to human consciousness . . . Hod is essentially the sphere of forms ensouled by the forces of Nature; and conversely, it is the sphere in which the forces of Nature take on sensible form.[48]

It is in Hod that the primal forces of Netzach are focused and concentrated into forms. In the practice of Hermetic magic that Fortune is describing here, the magician utilizes her will to contact the natural forces in Netzach and condense them into individual forms. But this process also works on the macrocosmic level, in which Hod is the sphere in which the energies of Netzach are categorized into specific identities. Hod thus has some similarities with Chokmah, the wisdom of God or the One Idea, on a lower level—it is a blueprint for all the forms that will take astral being in Yesod. Regardie writes, "It will help the student not a little if he remembers that the sphere of Hod represents on a very much lower plane similar qualities to those obtaining in Chokmah."[49]

On a sociopolitical or mesocosmic level, Hod is the sphere of civic bureaucracy. Hod is the sphere in which a society begins to regulate the inchoate social forces of the marketplace into an organized structure, in order to ensure the rights and needs of a society's citizens. The social Hod relies on the intellect, on a competent civil structure that can categorize, organize, and regulate social forces for the commonweal of all. Take, for example, the

---

48. Fortune, *Mystical Qabalah*, 230–31.
49. Regardie, *Garden of Pomegranates*, 60.

subway system of New York City, in which a complex and messy conglomeration of competing private subway lines was eventually made a public utility and regulated for the civic good of the city. Without this regulation and centralization, the system would never be able to operate 24/7, serving millions of New Yorkers and visitors on a daily basis.

Of course, this is the ideal Hod, the unfallen Hod. Bureaucracy is often a dirty word for a reason—in our fallen world, bureaucratic societies are frequently corrupt or incompetent. To take the example just given—the New York City subway system—we have seen a rapid deterioration in the functioning of the system over the last decade, due to a combination of civic incompetence, a lack of funding, and environmental disasters. But the answer is not to reprivatize the system, as some libertarian or conservative commentators have suggested. It is to bring Hod, the civic bureaucracy, back into balance with an organized and planned marketplace, all under the supremacy of the commonweal, or public good. It is thus that we translate the macrocosmic and microcosmic insights of the Tree of Life into the mesocosmic realm of human society, even for something as pedestrian or materialistic as a subway system.

IX. Yesod—Popular Culture

Yesod, as mentioned above, corresponds to popular culture—possibly the most traditional interpretation of a sephira below the supernal triad in our social Qabalah. This is because Yesod, the sphere of the Moon, is considered to be the astral world in the Hermetic Qabalah, the place of aether or *Akasha* depending on one's terminology and tradition. According to Regardie:

> Yesod is that subtle basis upon which the physical world is based . . . it is the Astral Plane, which in one sense being passive and reflecting the energies from above, is lunar, even as the moon reflects the light from the sun. The Astral Light is an omnipresent and all-permeating fluid or medium of extremely subtle matter; substance in a highly tenuous state, electric and magnetic in

constitution, which is the model upon which the physical world is built. It is the endless, changeless, ebb and flow of the world's force that, in the last resort, guarantees the stability of the world and provides its foundation. Yesod is this stable foundation, this changeless ebb and flow of astral forces, and the universal reproductive power in Nature... The general conception of Yesod is of change with stability. Some writers have referred to the Astral Light which is the sphere of Yesod as the Anima Mundi, the Soul of the World. The psycho-analyst Jung has a very similar concept which he terms the Collective Unconscious which, as I see it, differs in no wise from the Qabalistic idea.[50]

Yesod is where the inchoate powers of Netzach, given definition by the intellect of Hod, receive a form through the trappings of the astral light—the subtle matter that constitutes the entities commonly labeled ghosts or spirits in popular occultism, but which also clothes the incorporeal but still substantial entities labeled deities, angels, and other thought-forms. Yesod, in microcosmic terms, is the collective unconscious—the treasure-house of images which contains the immaterial ideas, dreams, and fantasies of the human imagination. It is also the zone in which the magician does most of his or her work, as the manipulation of the astral matter of Yesod is the primary goal of most forms of ceremonial magic.

As the treasure-house of images, Yesod also contains the images of popular culture—that realm in which the cosmic powers and principalities incarnate as the trends, perspectives, and icons of our shared cultural storehouse. Popular culture can be whimsical and chaotic, but—especially in our late capitalist context in the United States of the twenty-first century—it is also heavily shaped and dictated by the marketplace, by advertising, and mass media. What we enjoy consuming in popular culture is not the pure choice of our rational minds, but in fact subject to the influence of the economic order. In other social contexts—such as the Stalinist era of the Soviet Union—when Hod, the civic bureaucracy, holds more sway than Netzach—popular culture might instead be

50. Ibid., 60–61.

largely dictated by state interests and political propaganda. In a healthy society—which is hard to come by in this era called the fall—this lower triangle of Netzach, Hod, and Yesod would work in harmony under the commonweal of Tiphareth, allowing for an economic order that served the needs of the people, a civic bureaucracy that ensured a strong and robust social democracy, and a popular culture that gave form to the desires of the marketplace and the ideals of the state, but would not be entirely dictated by either of them. Such a society would require the harmony of the lower sephiroth, the proper and just rule of Tiphareth over the clashing emphases of the inferior spheres.

X. Malkuth—The Earthly City

The earthly city is the tenth sephira, Malkuth, the sphere of Earth and of the four elements. Regardie writes that Malkuth is "the world of the four elements, matter in its entirety, and all the forms perceived by our five senses, summing up in a crystallization the former nine digits or series of ideas."[51] As a pendant to the other nine sephiroth, Malkuth gathers together and concentrates all the influences and powers of the rest of the Tree and manifests them in the form of the material universe. It is the Daughter, the "Inferior Mother," the Bride and the Virgin—the sphere that is linked to the biblical tale of the fall of Eve, but also to the redemption wrought by the new Eve, the Virgin Mary. The Malkuth of the fallen world is like a gemstone that fell out of a crown—in an unfallen Tree, Malkuth would be in the place of Daath, resulting in a perfectly balanced and symmetrical arrangement of the spheres. In our fallen world, however, Malkuth is Eve exiled from the Garden of Eden—the site of the fallen souls, or *Neshamoth*. Yet a spark of the divine remains in Malkuth, pointing the way to the path of return to union with God. Regardie writes,

> In Malkuth, the lowest of the Sephiroth, the sphere of the physical world of matter, wherein incarnate the

---

51. Ibid., 62.

exiled *Neschamoth* from the divine palace, there abides the Shechinah, the spiritual Presence of Ain Soph as a heritage to mankind and an ever-present reminder of spiritual verities. That is why there is written "Kether is in Malkuth, and Malkuth is in Kether, though after another manner." The *Zohar* would imply that the real Shechinah, the real Divine Presence, is allocated to Binah whence it never descends, but that the Shechinah in Malkuth is an eidolon or Daughter of the Great Supernal Mother.[52]

Malkuth is, in the symbolism of the Zelator grade of the Golden Dawn (ascribed to Malkuth on the Tree of Life), the Tree of the Knowledge of Good and Evil. The Zelator initiation ritual states that

> from Gedulah [another name for Chesed] it [Malkuth] derives an influx of Mercy, and from Geburah an influx of Severity, and the Tree of the Knowledge of Good and of Evil shall it be until it is united with the Supernals in Daath.[53]

In this statement, the qabalistic redemption myth is recounted in a concise form: Malkuth will remain the unredeemed earthly city, the Tree of the Knowledge of Good and Evil from which temptation and the fall into profane materialism and sin emerges, until it is united with the supernal triad of Kether, Chokmah, and Binah in the place of Daath above the Abyss.

This process works through the raising of Malkuth, the Daughter, to the throne of Binah, the Mother, through the arousal of Chokmah, the Father—the joining of wisdom and understanding—leaving one in Daath, the invisible sephira of knowledge. Frater Achad writes,

> Had the Qabalistic Plan ended with the production of Malkuth the Kingdom or Material Universe, we should have been forced to admit that the Creative process was one of degeneration. And so it must appear to us from our limited viewpoint, until we have learned the Plan of

---

52. Ibid., 62.
53. Regardie, *Golden Dawn*, 145.

Redemption and profited by it . . . The Daughter must marry the Son and so become the Mother, true mate of the Father, before all is re-absorbed into the Crown of Light.[54]

Eschatologically speaking, we are talking about the marriage of the Earthly Bride with the Heavenly Bridegroom, "the holy city, the new Jerusalem, coming down out of heaven from God, prepared as a bride adorned for her husband."[55] This is the manifestation of the Holy City, which includes the transfiguration of the material cosmos—not just the individual person or human beings, but *the whole material cosmos*—into the kingdom of God on earth. This is the final step of the cosmic process, the great initiation begun by Eve when she ate the fruit of the Tree of the Knowledge of Good and Evil in the garden.

Until this process is complete, the earthly city of Malkuth will remain the unbalanced and fallen sphere of contending powers and principalities. The earthly city in our social Qabalah is the teeming city, the late capitalist dystopia of our urban nightmares. In the unredeemed Malkuth of our fallen world, the earthly city contains the confused and toxic cultural by-products (Yesodic forces) that come from the unbalanced powers of the rest of the Tree—corrupt bureaucracies, uncaring economic systems, and an insipid popular culture. But by progressive initiation and evolution—in other words, by the equilibrium of forces and the marriage of Malkuth the Daughter with Tiphareth the Son, the social commonweal—the earthly city is raised to the currently empty place of the quasi-sephira Daath. In this new, balanced location in the Tree of Life, the earthly city is transfigured into the New Jerusalem, the Heavenly City, or—in the parlance of our social Qabalah—the City of the Silver Star. And thus "all is re-absorbed into the Crown of Light."

---

54. Achad, *Egyptian Revival*, 16.
55. Rev 21:2 (NRSV).

Liberation

III

The True Grand Orient

> ... a recognition of Christ as the true Grand Orient, the Sun of Righteousness, who rises in the east to enlighten, employ and instruct the world.
>
> —C.W. Leadbeater[1]

A FEW YEARS BACK, I attended a Christmas Eve Mass at the Episcopal Cathedral of the Incarnation in Garden City, New York. Hanging above the high altar, shining brightly with silvery white light, was a large, glowing ornament of the Star of Bethlehem—a common decoration for the Advent season, but one that struck me with particular resonance as we walked up the aisle for Communion. As we celebrated the Christmas story, including the homage paid to the newborn savior at the manger in Bethlehem, we liturgically reenacted the journey of the magi by following the star ourselves to its fateful end—the real presence of Jesus Christ at the altar of the Eucharist.

According to orthodox sacramental theology, our journey to the high altar was not a mere dramatic portrayal of the real journey of the shepherds and the magi to the incarnate Christ in the manger—it was an actual journey to the sacramental presence of the Christ in the bread and wine of the Eucharist. Theologically speaking, the Eucharist is the avenue of our participation in the incarnation, crucifixion, and resurrection of Jesus Christ. The sacrament allows us to really enter the reality of the Christ event, especially the event of Calvary. As the *Catechism of the Catholic Church* explains, the Eucharist "*re-presents* (makes present) the sacrifice of

---

1. Leadbeater, *Science of the Sacraments*, 132.

the cross"; "the sacrifice of Christ and the sacrifice of the Eucharist are *one single sacrifice.*"[2] Every eucharistic celebration *is* the reality of Christ's presence, because the Christ event—his coming in the incarnation, his death on the cross, and the resurrection of his body—is an eschatological reality, the originary event of the new cosmos, "stretching vertically to the spiritual and horizontally to the physical, and meeting at the absurdity point, the point of the Christ who fully exists on both planes. There is no space that it does not touch."[3] The Eucharist, as theurgical re-presentation of the Christ event in our present day life, thus dissolves the "dualism between material and spiritual, divine and earthly."[4] As Elizabeth Stuart concludes, through the Eucharist "all and everything are caught up in this great drama of salvation."[5]

In a similar vein, the Eucharist also absorbs all other theurgical practices into the "great drama of salvation" inaugurated by Christ. Radical orthodox theologian John Milbank suggests that the theurgical reality of Christ's incarnation, represented in Christian practice by the Eucharist, in fact situates and authorizes all other theurgical—better known in contemporary occult parlance as "high magical"—practices and rituals:

> [T]he Christian fulfillment of theurgy as the descent of God himself in order to provide the true worship of himself impossible to fallen humanity in order to unleash his power of love in the world is able to appreciate and situate all the other "theurgic" attempts to captivate divine power in order to heal finite reality.[6]

Esotericists and occultists in the West, writing and practicing in a Christian context even if they refuse or condemn traditional Christian faith, often implicitly accept this formulation of the magical, theurgical power of the incarnate Christ in the Eucharist. C.

---

2. *Catechism of the Catholic Church*, 1366–1367.
3. Stuart, "Making No Sense," 117.
4. Ibid., 121.
5. Ibid., 121.
6. Milbank, "Foreword," 18–19.

W. Leadbeater, a leader in the Theosophical Society and bishop in the Liberal Catholic Church, devoted his treatise *The Science of the Sacraments* to the esoteric interpretation of the seven sacraments, and to the psychic manifestations that he could discern during the performance of the Eucharist. He alludes to Christ as the theurgical centerpoint of the cosmos in a passage on the eastward direction of the church (which also gives this chapter its title):

> In our Services [turning toward the east] means always a special endeavour to pour force outward and upward—a direct ascription of glory to God, in which the whole congregation joins, and a recognition of Christ as the true Grand Orient, the Sun of Righteousness, who rises in the east to enlighten, employ and instruct the world.[7]

Meanwhile, Papus, the late-nineteenth-century French occultist and founder of the Martinist Order, suggests that the Mass is a "purely Magical Ceremony," esoterically achieving the "evolution" of the mortal and natural world toward the divine, and the "involution" of the divine into the world.[8] During the eucharistic consecration, "the Divine Word rushes forth from the highest heavens to be united with the matter offered as sacrifice," and through his benediction the priest "unites the congregation with the symbolic receptacle of Divinity"—thus accomplishing anew the "incarnation of the Universal Spirit in the Celestial Virgin," the descent of Spirit into elemental matter.[9]

The Star of Bethlehem, then, as an icon of the incarnate Christ, the sign which the magi followed to pay homage to the newborn Jesus, represents a reordering of the cosmos around the True Grand Orient or the Star in the East, the Christ child whose status as the incarnation means that all the fallen powers and principalities of the world have been reconciled to their true *telos*, the manifestation of the One Idea or Word of God. Stringfellow, the

---

7. Leadbeater, *Science of the Sacraments*, 132.
8. Papus, *Elementary Treatise on Practical Magic*, 318.
9. Ibid., 320.

theologian of the cosmic powers and principalities, describes the Christmas story this way:

> [T]he manger scene itself is a political portrait of the whole of creation restored in the dominion of Jesus Christ in which every creature, every tongue and tribe, every rule and authority, every nation and principality is reconciled in homage to the Word of God incarnate.
>
> Amid portents and events such as these, commemorated customarily in the church, the watchword of Christmas—"peace on earth"—is not a sentimental adage but a political utterance and an eschatological proclamation, indeed, a preview and precursor of the Second Coming of Christ the Lord, which exposes the sham and spoils of the power of the rulers of this age.[10]

This cosmic-political interpretation of the Star of Bethlehem and the manger scene was echoed by the patristic theologians of Christian late antiquity, who saw the Star as a symbol of the reorientation of the magical universe (labeled by the church fathers as demonic) and all its pagan divinities around Christ the Lord, just as the Eastern magi reoriented themselves around the manger. Albert Pike, the nineteenth-century American Masonic scholar (himself influenced by many esoteric and occult sources, prominently including Eliphas Lévi), described this concept succinctly in his magnum opus, *Morals and Dogma of the Ancient and Accepted Scottish Rite of Freemasonry*:

> The advent of Christ was announced by a Star from the East; and His nativity was celebrated on the shortest day of the Julian Calendar, the day when, in the physical commemorations of Persia and Egypt, Mithras or Osiris was newly found. It was then that the acclamations of the Host of Heaven, the unfailing attendants of the Sun, surrounded, as at the spring-dawn of creation, the cradle of His birth-place, and that, in the words of Ignatius, "a star, with light inexpressible, shone forth in the Heavens, to destroy the power of magic and the bonds of wickedness;

---

10. Stringfellow, *William Stringfellow*, 52–53

for God Himself had appeared, in the form of man, for the renewal of eternal life."[11]

Christian esotericists like Pike, Lévi, and Papus agreed with this notion of the church fathers in outline; where they differed was in the place of the powers and principalities following the Advent of Christ. Like Stringfellow and Milbank, Christian esotericists and occultists believed that the theurgical and magical powers of the world were created by God to manifest God's intention for God's creation; Christ's incarnation repaired the fall that had left these powers in disarray, reconciling and reorienting them around the True Grand Orient. As Milbank suggests, the Eucharist, as the advent of Christ's real presence in the everyday theurgical practice of the Christian, becomes the magical rite *par excellence* around which all other rites of magic or theurgy now revolve, like planets orbiting the sun.

Just how does the coming of Christ reorient the cosmos? As we saw in our reflection on the social Qabalah, the One Idea of God for God's creation—a cosmos (and society) in which all things are ordered around the commonweal, operating in tandem for the peace and justice of all creatures—becomes incarnate in Jesus Christ, the "concentrated creation"[12] of God's intention for the universe, to use Schillebeeckx's striking phrase. In one of his earlier works, *Christ the Sacrament of the Encounter with God*, Schillebeeckx elaborates on how Jesus Christ is the "primordial sacrament,"[13] the originary sacrament from which the seven sacraments of the church emanate, not unlike the way the sephiroth of the Tree of Life emanate from the sephira of Kether, or the way the primary colors emanate from the Divine White Brilliance. According to Schillebeeckx, God constantly reaches out in grace to God's creation with the invitation to join in with God's intention for the universe; however, since creation is fallen, it constantly fails to respond to God's invitation—creation remains in disorder and

---

11. Pike, *Morals and Dogma*, 511.
12. Schillebeeckx, *Interim Report on the Books*, 128.
13. Schillebeeckx, *Christ the Sacrament*, 13.

death. But in Jesus Christ, the God-Man, "there was achieved the perfection both of the divine invitation and of the human response in faith from the man who by his resurrection is the Christ."[14]

Schillebeeckx sees grace as being both an inward and outward reality; only when the inward experience of grace—which is built into creation from the ground up—comes into dialogue with the "external address"[15] of God does it manifest as public revelation. The incarnate Christ is the fullness of revelation because in him both the "divine invitation," constituting the external address, and the internal "human response in faith"[16] are perfectly realized. Thus every human action of Christ was always "an offering of grace in a human form," and because these offerings appear "in visible form, the saving activity of Jesus is *sacramental.*"[17] Christ is therefore the "primordial sacrament"[18] from which the church's sacraments extend. And according to Milbank and the Christian esotericists, it is from the church's sacraments—specifically the Eucharist, as the sacrament of Christ's presence—that the magical rites of the rest of the world emanate; it is from the one divinity that the rest of the divinities of the world receive their power.

Put another way, because Jesus Christ is the incarnate Word of God or the incarnation of the One Idea, he—and the eucharistic sacrament that extends from him—is a pure vehicle for the impartation of the light of God to the rest of the cosmos. Indeed, in the theurgy of the primordial sacrament of Christ, the whole cosmos is caught up and transmuted into the One Idea of God, just as the bread and wine of the Eucharist are transubstantiated into the body and blood of the Son of God. In one of the rituals of his Fellowship of the Rosy Cross, A. E. Waite describes this cosmic process in occult terms by using the alchemical concept of the fifth element of spirit ruling over the four elements of the material world: "In the centre of all is the White Wheel of the Spirit, the

14. Ibid., 13.
15. Ibid., 13.
16. Ibid., 13.
17. Ibid., 14–15.
18. Ibid., 13.

Sign of the Cosmic Christ, of the Second Birth and the Christ-Life in Man."[19] This spirit wheel, by descending into matter (an esoteric description of the incarnation of Christ), frees humanity from the inexorable life of the elements, that disordered fate to which the material universe is subject because of the fall:

> [T]he Four Sacramental Elements of which man is said to have been made—which were gathered by the Elohim from the Four Quarters of Heaven, and are analogous to the parts of our personality—will be ruled as a kingdom by those who obey the Law, or—in other words—that man is detached by sanctity from the bondage of elemental life. But that by which he is liberated is the Wheel of the Spirit, dwelling in the centre of his personality.[20]

To be transmuted in this way, to internalize the "Wheel of the Spirit . . . in the centre of his personality," the adept or mystic must first undergo the same process as that which Jesus Christ underwent—the crucifixion. This self-sacrifice—which orthodox theology states is represented in the eucharistic ceremony—causes the aspirant to die to his lower self, allowing the divine light to pass through him into the world without any impurities to block its circulation. As Waite puts it in his ritual, "the Adept is crucified to his lower self-centre, and to that which is perishable in the world, for the manifestation of the Divine within him."[21]

Pierre Teilhard de Chardin's cosmic vision of Christ as the Omega Point, the cosmic Eucharist into which the whole universe is being integrated and transformed, provides a powerful image for this process and its sacramental, theurgical resonance.[22] In his seminal work, *The Divine Milieu*, Teilhard de Chardin describes

---

19. Waite, *Third Order of the Rosy Cross*, 30.
20. Ibid., 30.
21. Ibid., 31.
22. Juan Luis Segundo, a major Latin American liberation theologian from the generation after Teilhard, adapted Teilhard's concept of the Omega Point for liberation theology in his *A Theology for Artisans of a New Humanity*. We will examine Segundo's use of Teilhard's cosmic theology in chapter 6, "City of the Silver Star."

purity as a state of spiritual transparency or translucence, reached by those who seek "to give Christ's desire to consummate all things precedence over [their] own immediate and momentary advantage."[23] Still purer are those who, attracted by God, succeed "in giving that movement and impulse of Christ's an ever greater continuity, intensity and reality."[24]

Thus, according to Teilhard de Chardin, the purity of a being is "measured by the degree of the attraction that draws them towards the divine centre, or, what comes to the same thing, by their proximity to the centre."[25] For Teilhard de Chardin, the divine light is present everywhere and always drawing creation toward its center, the sacred heart of Christ, the Omega Point, or the beatific vision of God. To be pure, then, is to be close to the divine center, and to be drawn thusly means a person has become transparent to spirit; those who are close to union with God have cooperated with God's grace to increase their "transparency," allowing "the divine light, that never ceases to press in upon us," to "irrupt the more powerfully."[26]

One sees a clear parallel here with the theology of Merwin-Marie Snell, the founder and first Mahaguru of the Universal Brotherhood, in his essay "Transcendental Monism"—indeed, Teilhard de Chardin is probably the most prominent Catholic theologian whose doctrines are the closest to Snell's and the Universal Brotherhood's. In his essay, Snell describes the final result of cosmic evolution on the material creation as "perfect docility and transparency to spirit, through and in which it will return to God."[27] This squares well with Teilhard de Chardin's concept of the eschatological Omega Point, described in *The Divine Milieu*, in which the material creation—including our physical bodies—is divinized and made one with the body of the incarnate

---

23. Teilhard de Chardin, *Divine Milieu*, 107.
24. Ibid., 107.
25. Ibid., 108.
26. Ibid., 108.
27. Snell, "Transcendental Monism," 10.

Christ, the God-Man or *theanthropos* in the Greek term used by the Universal Brotherhood.

The model and exemplar of this divinization in Christian theology is the Virgin Mary, the *Theotokos*, or Mother of God. In mystical terms, according to Teilhard de Chardin, the Annunciation—the conception of the Virgin through the overshadowing of the Holy Spirit, announced to Mary by the Archangel Gabriel—is the mystery that illustrates how Mary of Nazareth conceived the incarnate Word in herself through achieving complete purity or "perfect docility and transparency to spirit":

> When the time had come when God resolved to realise his incarnation before our eyes, he had first of all to raise up in the world a virtue capable of drawing him as far as ourselves. He needed a mother who would engender him in the human sphere. What did he do? He created the Virgin Mary, that is to say he called forth on earth a purity so great that, within this transparency, he would concentrate himself to the point of appearing as a child. There, expressed in its strength and reality, is the power of purity to bring the divine to birth among us.[28]

In other words, Mary's purity and transparency to spirit was so great, so utterly perfect, that the divine light was able to become concentrated in her to such a degree that it became incarnate in the form of a child, the Christ child. This is the physical manifestation of the "concentrated creation" of which Schillebeeckx speaks. Mystically speaking, this story is a parable of how we, too, might become transparent to spirit enough to conceive the incarnate Word within us—a point not missed on those mystics who emphasize how all Christians, not just the Virgin Mary, must give birth to the Christ child within themselves. As the medieval mystic Meister Eckhart preached,

> If someone were to ask me: why do we pray, why do we fast, why do we all perform our devotions and good works, why are we baptized, why did God, the All-Highest, take on our flesh?—then I would reply: in order that

---

28. Teilhard de Chardin, *Divine Milieu*, 109.

THE INNER CHURCH IS THE HOPE OF THE WORLD: LIBERATION

God may be born in the soul and the soul born in God
... the Eternal Word is spoken internally in the heart of
the soul, in the most interior and purest part.[29]

Teilhard de Chardin further summarizes this idea in a letter from December 5, 1916, where he elucidates the meaning of the Immaculate Conception—the pure, sinless conception of Mary by her parents, free from the stain of original sin—in terms of his cosmic theology:

> For me the Immaculate Conception is the feast of "passive action," the action that functions simply by the transmission through us of divine energy. Purity in spite of outward appearances, is essentially an active virtue, because it concentrates God in us and on those who are subject to our influence. In our Lord, all modes of lower, restless, activity disappear within this single, luminous, function of drawing God to oneself, of receiving him and letting him penetrate one's being. To be active in such a way and such a degree, our Lady must have been brought into existence in the very heart of grace—for no later justification, no matter how immediate, could replace this constitutive, inborn, perfection of the purity that watched over the birth of her soul. It is thus that I see the Immaculate Conception. May the Lord give you and me too, a little of her translucence, which is so favorable to God's action.[30]

As the last line makes clear, although Mary was given this perfection of purity through a special dispensation from the Lord, we too are meant to develop something of this spiritual translucence in order to draw God to ourselves, to receive God and let God penetrate our being. Achieving this mystical state is the microcosmic equivalent of the grand consummation that will render the whole cosmos docile and transparent to spirit—the Omega Point in Teilhard de Chardin's thought and the providential fulfillment taught by Snell's Universal Brotherhood.

29. Eckhart, *Selected Writings*, 112–13.

30. Teilhard de Chardin, Letter of December 5, 1916, *Making of a Mind*, 149.

Teilhard de Chardin's cosmic vision of the Omega Point appears radical at first, but in fact it recapitulates a longtime theme in both the patristic theology of the incarnation and in Western esotericism: the deification, or *theosis*, of the believer, made possible by the incarnation of the Word. This is summarized in Irenaeus's famous formula, "God became man so that man could become god." But church fathers like Maximus the Confessor didn't stop there—in fact, the whole cosmos is to be deified, the fall repaired through the process begun in Christ, and creation glorified in a final consummation. This overlaps with Western esotericism's embrace of a microcosm-macrocosm cosmology, in which the human being—as microcosm—represents and mirrors the whole universe—as macrocosm—and, as the only creature that contains all the parts of earth and heaven, is the creature singly responsible for the recapitulation of the cosmos in God. As Norman Russell summarizes the doctrine,

> Deification is a major theme in Maximus... The kenosis of the Word is followed by the theosis of the believer, God's accommodation to the constrictions of human life by man's expansion, within the limitations of his creaturely capacity, to the infinity of the divine life. Deification is not simply another expression for salvation, the repair of the damage done by sin. It is the final end of salvation, the attainment of the destiny originally intended for humankind that Adam had in his grasp and threw away. It may be anticipated in some degree in this life, but it reaches its fulfilment in the next in the fullest possible union with the incarnate Word. It involves not only man but his whole world. For deification is in the end, the goal, the *skopos,* of the entire cosmos.[31]

The Rosicrucian Adeptus Minor grade of the Golden Dawn, in which the initiate births Christ within herself (like Mary) through the formula of 5=6—the microcosm joined to the macrocosm, the attainment of the Knowledge and Conversation of the Holy Guardian Angel, Higher Genius, or Christic self—is a dramatic

---

31. Russell on Maximus the Confessor, *Doctrine of Deification,* 262.

theurgical reenactment of this same process. This grade occurs qabalistically in the sphere of Tiphareth, the sphere corresponding to the Cosmic Christ, the commonweal of all creation according to our social Qabalah. The divine light of Teilhard de Chardin, especially in terms of his notion of spiritual purity or transparency, is thus similar to the formula of "light in extension" utilized in the Golden Dawn tradition, in which the initiate is gradually purified and made open to a greater and greater influx of divine light through the elemental initiations of the outer order—culminating in the Adeptus Minor ritual that initiates the candidate into the inner order, the R. R. et A. C., the Rose-Cross.

Thus Mary's role as the Immaculate Conception, the mesocosmic woman who joins microcosm to macrocosm, the pure creature whose immaculate heart is perfectly joined to the sacred heart of Christ, makes esoteric sense in terms of the Golden Dawn system, where the initiate unites his or her heart with the heart of Christ (the Higher Genius) while physically hanging on the cross of suffering. In traditional Catholic terms, this process is called Mary's Transfixion, her perfect participation in the sacrifice of Christ. And all Christians themselves participate in this sacrifice through the Eucharist, the one sacrifice of Calvary represented at the sacramental altar. Through this participation, the creature—whether it is a single initiate, human society, or the very planet itself—becomes transparent, emanating God's light to the rest of creation, becoming a healing force that works toward the reparation or Christification of the whole cosmos. The fallen powers and principalities become reoriented around the True Grand Orient, the Star of Bethlehem, the Cosmic Christ.

IV

The Silver Star of Bethlehem

> Thou, Star of the East, that didst conduct the Magi!
>
> Thou art The Same all-present in Heaven and in Hell!
>
> Thou that vibratest between the Light and the Darkness!
>
> Rising, descending! Changing ever, yet ever The Same!
>
> ... I invoke the priestess of the Silver Star ...
>
> —Aleister Crowley[1]

THE REORIENTATION OF THE cosmos around Jesus Christ, the True Grand Orient and Omega Point, the incarnate One Idea of God, is the good news of the Christian gospel. This reorientation touches all aspects of our lives, sacred and profane—it means that all harmful divinities and their magics are abrogate, with the fallen powers and principalities once again reconciled to their Creator and to God's true will for their being. As Stringfellow reminds us, these cosmic powers are not just supernatural entities, elemental spirits or deities from world mythology.[2] They are also the images, ideologies, and institutions of our human societies. Christ as the incarnate One Idea also means that God's blueprint for a harmonious society—one no longer ruled by the intertwined evils of racism, poverty, militarism, and ecological destruction, but instead liberated and ordered around the commonweal of all—is now the Omega Point of the presently corrupt and fallen society that we

---

1. Crowley, "Liber Israfel *sub figura LXIV*," paras. 13, 15.
2. Stringfellow, *Free in Obedience*, 64.

live in. We move everyday toward an era of integrality, in which "the arc of the universe bends toward justice."³

We have a responsibility as human beings to move this process along, to assist in the healing and evolution of our society along with Christ our repairer. And the cosmos itself, containing the diffuse divinities that have been reconciled to and reoriented around the Omega Point, wishes to assist us in our quest for universal reformation. Dr. King suggested many times that he felt that he and the civil rights movement had "cosmic companionship" in their work toward justice.⁴ In his "A Christmas Sermon on Peace," the final Christmas sermon he gave at Ebenezer Baptist Church before his assassination in the following year, King—in a paragraph reminiscent of our reflection in the previous chapter on Christ's nativity and sacrifice in the light of the deification of the universe—explicitly links the Christmas hope for peace with the darkness of the crucifixion on Good Friday, and ultimately with the Easter hope for resurrection that is shared by the rest of the cosmos:

> If there is to be peace on earth and good will toward men, we must finally believe in the ultimate morality of the universe, and believe that all reality hinges on moral foundations. Something must remind us of this as we once again stand in the Christmas season and think of the Easter season simultaneously, for the two somehow go together. Christ came to show us the way. Men love darkness rather than the light, and they crucified him,

---

3. "Integrality" is a keyword of the Universal Brotherhood, signifying that the Creator's intention for the cosmos is one of mutual relationship and integration.

4. Drew Dellinger writes that there is "an undiscovered Cosmological King, as evidenced by his frequent mentions of the stars and cosmos and invocations of the universe. From the beginning of his leadership King used language that was not only theological, but consistently cosmological. 'We have the strange feeling down in Montgomery that in our struggle for justice we have cosmic companionship,' he stated in the summer of 1956. Three months later, addressing a mass meeting at Holt Street Baptist Church, King reflected on the historic Bus Boycott: 'These eleven months have not at all been easy . . . Our feet have often been tired (Yes) and our automobiles worn, but we have kept going with the faith that in our struggle we have cosmic companionship, and that, at bottom, the universe is on the side of justice.'" Dellinger, "Ecological King," para. 13.

and there on Good Friday on the cross it was still dark, but then Easter came, and Easter is an eternal reminder of the fact that the truth-crushed earth will rise again. Easter justifies Carlyle in saying, "No lie can live forever." And so this is our faith, as we continue to hope for peace on earth and good will toward men: let us know that in the process we have cosmic companionship.[5]

In esoteric terms, this cosmic companionship is the inner church, the assembly of the elect who have been conformed to God's One Idea for the cosmos. The inner church is made possible by the process begun by Christ the repairer, the reorientation of the fallen cosmos and all its structures (including human societies) toward the Omega Point. We will reflect upon the doctrine of the inner church more deeply in the next chapter. Here it is necessary to state that, qabalistically, the inner or hidden church is located within the upper reaches of the Tree of Life, specifically in the quasi-sephira of Daath—what we labeled in our social Qabalah the City of the Silver Star. Conceptually speaking, here is where the heavenly city "whose Builder and Maker is God" is to be found, the worldly city (Malkuth) having been recapitulated through union with the commonweal (Tiphareth, the heart of Christ).[6]

In the Golden Dawn tradition that was extended and transformed by Aleister Crowley in his A∴A∴ system, this area of the Tree is ascribed to the third order, the Silver Star. Regardie writes, "In the old Rosicrucian grade system, the Supernal triad constitutes the Inner College of Masters, and is called the Order of the Silver Star."[7] If the first or outer order represents the purification process of the earthly elements of society, the worldly city of Malkuth, and the second order of the R. R. et A. C. or Rosy-Cross represents the *theosis* of the individual initiate, attained in the Tiphareth sphere of the cosmic Christ (as described in the previous chapter), then

---

5. King, *Trumpet of Conscience*, 77–78.

6. King, "State of the Movement (November 1967)," 12; cited in Wessel-McCoy, "'Freedom Church of the Poor,'" 232–33.

7. Regardie, *Garden of Pomegranates*, 70.

the third order or Silver Star represents the deification of the entire cosmos—the end goal or *skopos* of the cosmic process.

The entities of the Silver Star, known variously in different traditions as the Inner College of Masters, the inner or hidden church, the secret chiefs, the Great White Brotherhood, or the Unknown Superiors, work to assist humanity in the evolution of the cosmos and human society. The notion of hidden masters is one of the most common esoteric concepts. One occult encyclopedia defines the concept this way in an entry labeled "Secret Chiefs," making specific reference to its use in the Golden Dawn:

> One of the terms used to designate to a group of entities of superhuman intelligence and power referred to in several schools of the occult, and believed to be immortal transmitters of secret knowledge.
>
> Several schools of the occult have made claims to having been given secret knowledge by a mysterious group of entities of superhuman intelligence and power. These beings are variously believed to be discarnate spirits of the great Magi of the past, living Magi who can astrally project themselves, angels or discarnate ethereal spirits, and are thought by some to inhabit the unpopulated regions of Tibet. Macgregor Mathers, one of the founders of the Hermetic Order of the Golden Dawn, claimed to be in contact with them, and to be directly responsible to them; he called them the Secret Chiefs, and said that the ritual magic which he set down for the Golden Dawn was transmitted to him by them. The Golden Dawn consisted of an Outer and an Inner Order, and a third Order which Mathers said consisted solely of Secret Chiefs.[8]

Descriptions of these secret chiefs, this inner college of masters or unknown superiors, abounds in Western esoteric literature. A. E. Waite describes this assembly in terms of the Tree of Life in one of the grade rituals of his own Rosicrucian order:

> [I]n another form of symbolism, the Tree is itself the elect. The blessings which are poured continually upon

---

8. McGovern, *Chambers Dictionary of the Unexplained*, 613.

the outer world descend from it and from them. They are the Blessed Company in the Sanctuary of the Hidden Church. When the elect shall enter into perfect liberation, the whole world will be nourished by the Tree of Life, sustained and enlightened by SHEKINAH.[9]

David Cherubim, a Thelemite author, describes the secret chiefs "as the secret life and intelligence of the Third Order of the Hermit Grade, which is the Holy Order of the Silver Star."[10] And he links these beings with the evolutionary advancement of humanity and its societies:

> It is a fact of Magick that the higher you ascend the Tree of Initiation the more involved you become with the development of the all, that is, with humanity as a whole. Literally, you become a conscious and responsible part of the all, so that inevitably you become the all itself, and in this you become a center of great evolutionary power for the actual welfare of mankind.[11]

Paul Foster Case, an alumnus of the Alpha et Omega offshoot of the Golden Dawn and founder of Builders of the Adytum, summarizes the Order of the Silver Star and its headship in the incarnate Christ this way:

> The Grade of Ipsissimus [ascribed to the highest sphere of Kether] is that of the hand of the Invisible Order . . . The Supreme "Head" of the Order is none other than the Christos, the universal Logos. Below Him are the solar Logoi of the various planetary systems, and below these the Logoi, or spirits of separate planets. Among incarnate beings on any planets, the post of "Head" is occupied by that one among the Magi who has attained to the most perfect unification with the Primal Will. No man is appointed to this post, nor elected to it. The degree

---

9. Waite, *Grade of Practicus*, 37.
10. Cherubim, "Golden Dawn and the Secret," para. 4.
11. Ibid., para. 5.

of attainment is the only determining factor. And this degree is judged by no man. It simply IS.[12]

Case here describes the grade system of Rosicrucianism in terms of the reorientation of the cosmic powers around the True Grand Orient, the Christ, whose light is shed on the rest of the cosmos by the deified magi who have traversed the upward path to the Silver Star.

All powers and principalities, and all high magic or theurgy, is recapitulated in the light of the Silver Star of Bethlehem, the icon of the *Christos* or "universal Logos." Western esotericism, as a spiritual system that developed—at least in Europe and the United States—in the Christian world, contains traces of this doctrine even among the rituals and rites of its most ardently anti-Christian exemplars. To further illuminate the esoteric concept of the Silver Star, we will explore one example of this theurgical reality for the remainder of this chapter.

Liber Israfel *sub figura LXIV* is an A∴A∴ ritual published by Aleister Crowley in his magnum opus, *Magick*.[13] It is described in the "Official Instructions of the A∴A∴" as "An instruction in a suitable method of preaching."[14] In fact, the ritual is an invocation of the Egyptian god Thoth, an assumption of Thoth as a godform in order to channel a word or sermon from the supernal triad of the Tree of Life—from the inner college of masters or the secret chiefs. Crowley summaries the rhythm of the ritual in his *Liber ABA*:

> The magician addresses the God with an active projection of Will, and then remains passive and silent while the God addresses the Magician. Again in the third part the deified magician addresses the Universe and in the fourth part remains silent, listening to the prayer which arises therefrom.[15]

---

12. Case, *True and Invisible Rosicrucian Order*, 297.
13. Crowley, "Liber Israfel *sub figura LXIV*."
14. Crowley, *Magick*, 466.
15. Ibid., 150.

The ritual thus follows the same essential structure as Papus's esoteric description of the Catholic Eucharist—an evolution of the human toward the divine, followed by an involution of the divine toward the human. Papus uses the hexagram of the Star of Solomon as the symbol of this process: "Solomon's star perfectly expresses this double action of evolution and involution, of which the Mass is just a translation for our eyes."[16]

Crowley, meanwhile, comments that the rhythm of Liber Israfel "may also be classed under Tetragrammaton," the elemental formula of the Qabalah:

> The first part is fire, the eager prayer of the magician, the second water, in which the magician listens to, or catches the reflection of, the god. The third part is air, the marriage of fire and water; the god and the man have become one; while the fourth part corresponds to earth, the condensation or materialization of those three higher principles.[17]

This formula both reiterates Papus's reference to the hexagram for a ritual that involves evolution and involution—the upward pointing triangle represents the element of fire while the downward facing represents water—and connects Crowley's rite with the qabalistic redemption myth, as the four parts of Tetragrammaton also represent the Father, Mother, Son, and Daughter of Qabalah. The third part of the ritual, in which "the god and the man have become one," thus reflects the qabalistic Son, the incarnate Messiah of Tiphareth. The fourth part of the ritual, in which a Word from the supernals is made incarnate on the material plane, is a reflection of the raising of the Daughter—the earthly city of Malkuth—to the supernal triad. It is the eschatological result of the Word's incarnation on the material plane.

In verses 8 and 9 of the ritual, the magician moves from the sphere of Hod (associated with Mercury and Thoth, gods of communication) to the sphere of Tiphareth. Working within this solar sphere, situated along the middle pillar of the Tree of Life

16. Papus, *Elementary Treatise on Practical Magic*, 320.
17. Crowley, *Magick*, 150.

from Kether to Malkuth, requires the magician to take on the godform of Ra. As Otto Omicron explains in his commentary on the ritual, "It is necessary to align oneself so as to receive direct communication from the Godhead (Kether) which shall be sent through Asi (section 15) or the 13th path [of the Tree of Life]."[18] Entering Tiphareth here also aligns the magician with the Christ consciousness, the Son of God—the image of Kether, the Godhead, reflected over the Abyss:

> If I say "Come up upon the mountains!" the Celestial Waters shall flow at my Word.
>
> For I am Ra incarnate!
>
> Khephra created in the Flesh!
>
> I am the Eidolon of my father Tmu, Lord of the City of the Sun![19]

The symbolism of the twelfth verse, in which the magician requests the transmission to come to him or her from Kether follows: "Therefore do Thou come forth unto me from Thine abode in the Silence: Unutterable Wisdom! All-Light! All-Power!"[20] And again, after the invocation of the "priestess of the Silver Star, Asi the Curved One,"[21] in verse 15, through the "ritual of silence," the transmission from Kether expresses itself through the magician to the gathered congregation: "I make open the gate of Bliss; I descend from the Palace of the Stars; I greet you, I embrace you, O children of earth, that are gathered together in the Hall of Darkness."[22] Omicron explains:

> The "Priestess of the Silver Star" is Atu II or the High Priestess and also the path between Kether and Tiphareth. This is the connection necessary for the communication to be received "from on high." Asi is the

18. Omicron, "Commentary on Liber Israfel," para. 19.
19. Crowley, "Liber Israfel *sub figura LXIV*," para. 9.
20. Ibid., para. 12.
21. Ibid., para. 15.
22. Ibid., para. 16.

Goddess of the Sky & Heavens in ancient Palestine and is comparable with Nuit.[23]

Then follows the pause and the sign of silence (a key ritual gesture from the Hermetic Order of the Golden Dawn). Omicron again:

> The "Ritual of Silence" is enacted at section 17 and the magician pauses in silence with the Sign of Silence in order to "receive" the message of the Godhead. Previous to these sections the magician assumed the Thoth aspect which embodied the Speech function of the ceremony, now the position of the High Priestess is assumed which facilitates the silence. This in turn acts as the "blank slate" so the impression of the message may be received.[24]

Qabalistically speaking, the magician moves from Hod to Tiphareth (Thoth/Mercury to Ra in terms of godforms), and there receives the transmission from Kether—the Godhead, the Divine White Brilliance—along the path of *gimel*, the High Priestess in terms of the Tarot and the Priestess of the Silver Star according to the ritual. By this path, the divine transmission or word traverses the Abyss that separates the secret chiefs—who dwell in the light of the supernals—from terrestrial humanity, and it is received by the magician, who shares it with the congregation.

Liber Israfel provides us with several clues to understand Crowley's interpretation of a number of symbols pertinent to our study of the Silver Star of Bethlehem, and its role in the regeneration of the cosmos and of human society. The High Priestess, associated with the Hebrew letter *gimel* and thus with the path between Tiphareth and Kether over the Abyss, is also the Priestess of the Silver Star. The Silver Star, of course, is embedded in the name of Crowley's magical order the A∴A∴ (whether one believes the order's true name to be in Latin or Greek), and is the Silver Star of the third order that Crowley, unlike the original Golden Dawn, believed is reachable in this corporeal lifetime in the esoteric grades

---

23. Omicron, "Commentary, on Liber Israfel," para. 30.
24. Ibid., para. 30.

of 8=3 and above (which Crowley, of course, claimed in his own lifetime). The pathway of the Priestess of the Silver Star is thus the pathway of the secret chiefs of the third order, who dwell above the Abyss in the light of the supernal triad.

It would be a stretch to overemphasize the Christic nature of the ritual, which is of course inundated by Egyptian and Thelemic symbolism—but by invoking the Star of the Magi and linking it to the Silver Star of the third order, Crowley himself provides recourse to understand that Liber Israfel, beyond being a magical ritual to receive a divine word or transmission, is also a complex poetic account of the incarnation of *the* Word, the Logos of God and the incarnation of the One Idea, regardless of Crowley's conscious intentions. In other words, on the basis of Christian Qabalah, Liber Israfel is necessarily incarnational.

Crowley unpacks the symbolism of the Silver Star, identified here as the Star of the East—the Star of Bethlehem—in verse 13:

> Thou, Star of the East, that didst conduct the Magi!
>
> Thou art The Same all-present in Heaven and in Hell!
>
> Thou that vibratest between the Light and the Darkness!
>
> Rising, descending! Changing ever, yet ever The Same!
>
> The Sun is Thy Father!
>
> Thy Mother is the Moon!
>
> The Wind hath borne Thee in its bosom: and Earth hath ever nourished the changeless Godhead of Thy Youth![25]

Like the apocryphal *Revelation of the Magi*, Crowley seems to be identifying the Star of the East here with that to which it points, the Logos or Word of the Godhead, the reception of which is the purpose of the entire ritual. The Star of the East is identified with the Godhead, and its pronouns receive the capitalizations appropriate to God. The star is present in both heaven and hell (the Word of course descends to the depths in the harrowing of

---

25. Crowley, "Liber Israfel *sub figura LXIV*," para. 13.

hell following the crucifixion), rises and descends, changes but remains "The Same." The sun—the god Ra or the solar sphere of Tiphareth—is its father, and the moon—the path of *gimel* or the High Priestess, the Priestess of the Silver Star—is its mother. The wind—or the Holy Spirit—bears the Word over the Abyss to physical incarnation, and the Word is received by the Earth and the "children of earth," gathered together in the material world, the "Hall of Darkness" of verse 16.

And if the High Priestess, *gimel*, associated with the moon, is both mother of the Logos *and* Priestess of the Silver Star, this is because the High Priestess is also a symbol of the Virgin Mary, who conceives the Logos through her overshadowing by the Holy Spirit—"The Wind hath borne Thee in its bosom,"[26] as Crowley explains. Crowley himself suggests the connection between the Virgin Mary and the High Priestess in his "On the Powers of Number":

> The Tarot Key is the High Priestess—but she is also Isis—the Catholic Church has grasped this dogma in great purity. The Virgin Mary, herself immaculate, formulates the Christ (in his aspect as Adam Qadmon the Universe undefiled) by the influx of the Divine Spirit or breath. By the Virgin do our prayers ascend unto the Throne... Now this card is the occult link between the human life and the Divine Light. The High Priestess is the Higher Soul of Man and his aspiration unto the Divine. The denial of the Virgin is therefore no less than the unpardonable sin: for it is the denial of the Holy Spirit in oneself.[27]

In other words, the Silver Star which is the Word of God—whose priestess is the immaculate Virgin Mary—finds incarnation as the Christ by the influx of the Holy Spirit, the descent of the divine light into the material world of human life. In qabalistic terms, this is the insertion of the Hebrew letter *shin*, representative of the hidden fifth element of spirit (the spirit wheel in alchemical symbolism), into the elemental formula of YHVH, the Tetragrammaton, which characterizes Assiah or the material plane. Recall

---

26. Crowley, "Liber Israfel *sub figura LXIV*," para. 13.
27. Crowley, "On the Powers of Number," 4.

that Crowley has already linked the structure of Liber Israfel to the Tetragrammaton. By inserting *shin*, the ritual moves from Tetragrammaton to Pentagrammaton, the qabalistic name of Jesus formulated by the Renaissance Christian Cabalists and central to many of the rituals of the Golden Dawn: *Yeheshuah*.

After this extended analysis of Crowley's Liber Israfel, two facts are now apparent: one, it is very difficult, even for an avowed anti-Christian occultist like Aleister Crowley, to truly transcend the heavily Christian symbolism of the Hermetic Qabalah, which found its genesis in the polemical Christian Cabala of the Renaissance; and two, the symbol of the Silver Star—the Star of the East, the Star of the Magi—is intimately bound up with the incarnation of the Logos, the reception in the material universe of the Word of God—the God-Man Yeheshuah, Jesus Christ, the One Idea of God made incarnate on this plane of manifestation.

Furthermore, if Yeheshuah is the Silver Star made incarnate in the material world, then his priestess and mother is Mary Immaculate, who formulates the Star of the East in her heart as the exemplar of the Western esoteric goal of *theosis*—the process of receiving the influx of the Holy Spirit, or the divine light, within oneself. For, as Crowley explains, if the Priestess of the Silver Star is the "Higher Soul of Man and his aspiration unto the Divine," then the denial of Mary Immaculate is "no less than the unpardonable sin . . . the denial of the Holy Spirit in oneself,"[28] the denial of the possibility of *theosis*. And as we saw in the cosmic doctrines of Teilhard de Chardin, Mary is also linked to the cosmos itself, the mesocosmic instrument that conceives the Word and thus begins the process of transmuting the universe, and human society, into the holy city. As Crowley exclaims to the Silver Star in the ritual, "Earth hath ever nourished the changeless Godhead of Thy Youth"—Mary as the qabalistic daughter, Malkuth, Earth, has nourished the Word of God in her womb, giving birth to the One Idea on the plane of manifestation. In other words, because of the primordial sacrament of the Silver Star, which situates all theurgical practices around its incarnate presence, the pure white light

---

28. Crowley, "On the Powers of Number," 4.

of the One Idea has been imparted to the material cosmos, transubstantiating it into the body and blood of the Cosmic Christ—transmuting the earthly city into the City of the Silver Star.

Consummation

V

The Inner Church

> Perhaps I must turn my faith to the inner spiritual church, the church within the church, as the true ekklesia and the hope of the world.
>
> —Rev. Dr. Martin Luther King Jr.[1]

MANY SCHOLARS RIGHTLY ASSOCIATE Rev. Dr. Martin Luther King Jr. with the black church, or with the liberal Protestantism of his seminary education. But as Peter Heltzel explains, Dr. King was also deeply influenced by the long tradition of radical pietism.[2] In the quote from his famous "Letter from a Birmingham Jail," King expresses his frustration with the organized churches, especially white moderate churches in the South, for suggesting that the Civil Rights Movement should exhibit more patience in the struggle for black freedom and justice. Because of the frustrating tepidity of the mainline church, King wonders if it would be better to place his hope elsewhere:

> Perhaps I must turn my faith to the inner spiritual church, the church within the church, as the true ekklesia and the hope of the world. But again I am thankful to God that some noble souls from the ranks of organized religion have broken loose from the paralyzing chains of conformity and joined us as active partners in the struggle for freedom."

---

1. King, "Letter from a Birmingham Jail," para. 34.
2. Heltzel, "Inner Church is the Hope," 269–81.

THE INNER CHURCH IS THE HOPE OF THE WORLD: CONSUMMATION

Heltzel contextualizes the reference here to the "inner spiritual church, the church within the church," within a genealogy tracing the influence of radical pietism on the black church tradition from which King draws much of his power and inspiration.³ Heltzel extends his history from the Puritans in the "New World" through the Moravians to the early Lutheran pietists, reaching back to Philipp Spener's important devotional text *Pia Desideria* and its influence on the development of small groups within the churches and its support for the spiritual priesthood of all believers, what Spener meant by the "church within the church."⁴ But Heltzel's genealogy stops here—he does not go further back to the esoteric roots of radical pietism. In fact, pietism shares a lineage with the Christian theosophy of the eighteenth century, both of which were heavily influenced by the Hermetic and Rosicrucian esotericisms of the early seventeenth century. Nicholas Goodrick-Clarke explains,

> Eighteenth-century theosophy is also related to Pietism, a widespread and influential reform movement from the late seventeenth century onward. This Lutheran movement traces its origins to Johann Arndt (1555–1621) whose *Vier Bücher vom warren Christenthum (Four Books of True Christianity)* (1605–1610) emphasized an interior, vital Christianity as opposed to a formal, rigid, and institutional variety. Arndt's book of edification contained key esoteric references, including Hermes Trismegistus, Paracelsus, and Valentin Weigel. Philipp Jakob Spener (1635–1705) was sympathetic to the writings of Boehme and gave the Pietist movement its manifesto with his work *Pia Desideria* (1675), which emphasized rebirth, renewal, and a personal form of Christianity. Spener achieved significant influence on appointment as senior court preacher at Dresden from 1686. Spener's famous pupil August Hermann Francke (1663–1727) combined zeal with practical vision and organizational ability at Halle, where his educational

---

3. Ibid., 269–81.
4. Ibid., 272–73.

foundation, orphanage, and pastoral training school were established. Radical Pietists such as Gottfried Arnold (1666–1714) often separated themselves from their original churches to found sects, and some were influenced strongly by Boheme's theosophy. A major example of separatism is the Moravian Church, deriving from the *Unitas Fratrum* associated with the name of Jan Amos Comenius (1592–1670), and refounded by Nicolaus Ludwig, Count Zinzendorf (1700–1760). However, in the duchy of Württemberg, the Protestant state of southwest Germany (Swabia), Pietism was characterized by a combination of biblical scholarship and theosophical speculation; its chief representatives being Johann Albrecht Bengal (1687–1752) and Friedrich Christoph Oetinger (1702–1782).

Given its emphasis on interior spirituality, Pietism fostered an intellectual atmosphere receptive to esotericism. During the first part of the eighteenth century, Hermeticism and alchemy were widespread in Germany.[5]

Many of the names that appear here are vanguards of Western esotericism and Rosicrucianism during the early modern period—Paracelsus, Valentin Weigel, Jacob Boehme, and Jan Amos Comenius (the last being a central figure in both the history of the Moravian church and in the pansophic and Rosicrucian esoteric movements of the seventeenth century). This fuller history of the esoteric roots of pietism contains a description that could apply to eighteenth-century theosophers as well as the radical pietists—an "interior, vital Christianity as opposed to a formal, rigid and institutional variety." The pietist "emphasis on interior spirituality"[6] describes well the doctrine of the inner church proposed by Christian theosophers such as Karl von Eckartshausen, Ivan Vladimirovich Lopukhin, and Louis Claude de Saint-Martin in the eighteenth century, all figures associated with Rosicrucian esotericism.

---

5. Goodrick-Clarke, *Western Esoteric Traditions*, 103–4.
6. Ibid., 103–4

R. A. Gilbert suggests that the "philosophy and ideals of the Rosicrucian movement reached the New World in 1694 when Johannes Kelpius and the first wave of German Pietists settled on the Wissahickon River in what is now a suburb of Philadelphia."[7] Gilbert thus draws a direct line between the radical pietists, including those who arrived in America in the late seventeenth century, and the Rosicrucian movement, which shared the pietist emphasis on the inner church, on interior spirituality, and on social reform. Christopher McIntosh describes Kelpius as "a man steeped in theosophical and millenialist ideas"; of his pietist group McIntosh concludes that "it is fair to say that the tenor of their philosophy and way of life has a flavour of the Rosicrucian tradition about it."[8] The history of pietism in America, helpfully traced in the lineage of Dr. King by Heltzel, thus contains a clear, if indirect, strain of Rosicrucian esotericism.

If Heltzel is accurate in identifying a pietist influence on Dr. King's concept of the inner spiritual church—the church within the church, the true *ekklesia*—then King's inner church also contains a germ of Rosicrucianism and Christian theosophy. In Eckartshausen's *The Cloud upon the Sanctuary*, the classic eighteenth-century Christian theosophical account of the inner or interior church—and a major influence on the Hermetic Order of the Golden Dawn, A. E. Waite, and Aleister Crowley—the inner church is described as

> that illuminated Community of God which is scattered throughout the world, but which is governed by one truth and united in one spirit. This enlightened community has existed since the first day of the world's creation, and its duration will be to the last day of time.[9]

The inner church is thus that communion of the Saints in light, that holy assembly of the secret chiefs or unknown superiors—the third order of the Silver Star, made possible by the reorientation

---

7. Gilbert, "Lost Stepchild," para. 1.
8. McIntosh, *Rosy Cross Unveiled*, 129–30.
9. Von Eckartshausen, *Cloud upon the Sanctuary*, 33.

of the cosmos begun with the event of Christ—which leads humanity on the path of return to union with God and to harmony with all of creation.[10] As Eckartshausen says, the interior church "was formed immediately after the fall of man, and received from God at first-hand the revelation of the means by which fallen humanity could be again raised to its rights and delivered from its misery."[11] The members of the interior church are "united in truth, and their Chief is the Light of the World himself, Jesus Christ, the One Anointed in light, the single mediator for the human race."[12] But the feebleness of fallen humanity required an outward veil for the inward grace of the inner church. According to Eckartshausen, this is the origin of the external church, the church as an institution and a bureaucracy:

> [T]he frailty of man and his weakness necessitated an exterior society which veiled the interior one, and concealed the spirit and the truth in the letter ... Therefore, interior truths were wrapped in external and perceptible ceremonies, so that men, by the perception of the outer, which is the symbol of the interior, might by degrees be enabled safely to approach the interior spiritual truths.[13]

Unlike the exterior church, the inner church transcends institutional boundaries, geographical borders, and exterior divisions; it is "composed of scattered members, but tied by the bonds of perfect unity and love," and has been occupied "from the earliest

---

10. Aleister Crowley was deeply impressed by Eckartshausen's book, which was recommended to him by A. E. Waite, and he entered the Hermetic Order of the Golden Dawn in 1898 precisely to find the interior church of which Eckartshausen speaks. Later, he would adapt letter II of *The Cloud upon the Sanctuary* into Liber XXXIII, *An Account of the A∴ A∴*—his Order of the Astrum Argenteum or the Silver Star—by changing the references to Jesus Christ in the original text to references about himself, and changing all instances of the word "God" to "L. V. X."

11. Eckartshausen, *Cloud upon the Sanctuary*, 35.

12. Ibid., 34. Eckartshausen's light-centered language about Christ here is very similar to the concepts explored in chapters 3–4.

13. Ibid., 35.

ages in building the grand Temple through the regeneration of humanity, by which the reign of God will be manifest."[14]

The lofty esotericism of these quotations from Eckartshausen might seem to render his doctrine of the inner church remote from that of Dr. King. But there are many similarities. Like Eckartshausen, King suggests that the exterior church—to which he ascribes the church of the white moderates who opposed the Civil Rights Movement's recourse to civil disobedience in Birmingham—often clouds the true Christianity of the inner church, which transcends institutional borders and bureaucratic niceties. King agrees that it is the inner church, the true *ekklesia*, which preserves the intention of God for creation, and directs humanity back on the path to harmony with the divine.[15] And King agrees that the external church often debases the inner church, selling the spirit for the letter, and that this causes the external church to lose all moral authority, just as the white moderate churches did in Birmingham. Compare this to Eckartshausen, who explains that though the external church "was visible, the interior Church . . . always invisible," the inner church "yet must govern all, because force and power are alone confided to her."[16] The exterior church itself fell when "the divine external worship abandoned the interior worship."[17]

The only difference between King's pietist concept of the inner spiritual church, "the church within the church," and the esoteric interior church of Eckartshausen, is that King associates belonging to the inner church with espousing a liberative gospel of freeing the oppressed and the marginalized—a political-spiritual orientation toward the pietist mysticism whose language he draws upon. It is not enough for an individual Christian to seek interior union with God in a safe, private place, away from the snares and

---

14. Ibid., 34.

15. In "Letter from a Birmingham Jail," King writes that it is the witness of those who have joined the black freedom struggle—those who have joined the inner spiritual church—that "has been the spiritual salt that has preserved the true meaning of the gospel in these troubled times" (para. 34).

16. Eckartshausen, *Cloud upon the Sanctuary*, 39.

17. Ibid., 39.

oppressions of human society. If someone is truly a member of that invisible assembly that Eckartshausen compares to "the Communion of Saints in light," they must be willing to directly engage with the unjust and fallen powers of this world to bring God's kingdom to earth as it is in heaven. This includes unjust and fallen social structures. After all, this is what Jesus Christ did, even unto the suffering of the cross, and the church—born during the crucifixion—is nothing other than the sacramental body of Christ in human history: "The cross is the revelation of the extent to which God was willing to go in order to restore broken humanity."[18] The inner church, if it is really the church, must share in this commitment. As King writes, "The projection of a social gospel, in my opinion, is the true witness of a Christian life. This is the meaning of the true *ekklesia*—the inner spiritual church."[19]

Like Eckartshausen's interior church, King's true *ekklesia* contains members from many different denominations and religions, and from no religion at all, because to be a member of it you must simply align yourself—and your spirituality, your way of living in the world—with God's peaceable One Idea for human society. But in his later years, while organizing the Poor People's Campaign of 1967–68, King also clarified his concept of the inner church in a way that took him from social gospel to liberation theology: by incorporating the preferential option for the poor into his vision of what the inner spiritual church must look like. According to Latin American liberation theologians like Gustavo Gutiérrez, who influenced the use of the phrase at the 1979 Puebla Conference in Mexico, the preferential option for the poor refers to "God's predilection for those on the lower rung of the ladder of history."[20] Against liberation theology's critics, Gutiérrez locates this doctrine in the Bible itself:

> In the final analysis, an option for the poor is an option for the God of the kingdom whom Jesus proclaims to us ... The entire Bible, beginning with the story of Cain and

18. Kairos Center, "When Jesus Says Love," para. 8.
19. King, "Where Do We Go from Here?," 345.
20. Gutiérrez, *Theology of Liberation*, xxvi.

Abel, mirrors God's predilection for the weak and abused of human history. This preference brings out the gratuitous or unmerited character of God's love. The same revelation is given in the evangelical Beatitudes, for they tell us with the utmost simplicity that God's predilection for the poor, the hungry, and the suffering is based on God's unmerited goodness to us.[21]

Like the Latin American liberation theologians, the Dr. King of the Poor People's Campaign determined that it was the poor and dispossessed of our society who must receive the "preferential option"; in order to be true to the God of the Bible, it was the struggles of the poor and the leadership of the poor that must be centered in the movement for social justice. The poor *as a class* must lead the way to the "radical revolution of values" that our whole sick society requires to align itself with God's One Idea for the world; any other leadership will only reproduce our current social priorities, which privilege the few and the wealthy over the dispossessed. As Gutiérrez writes, "only when we opt preferentially for the poorest and weakest can we begin to display universality—anything less is tainted with the exclusive ways of present social structures."[22] By organizing the Poor People's Campaign, King declared that, if the inner spiritual church is made up of those people who have aligned themselves with the values of God's kingdom, the inner church must also be the "freedom church of the poor."[23] He proclaimed,

> I choose to identify with the underprivileged. I choose to identify with the poor. I choose to give my life for the hungry. I choose to give my life for those who have been left out . . . This is the way I'm going. If it means suffering

---

21. Ibid., xxvii.

22. Gutiérrez and Farmer, *In the Company of the Poor*, location 601 of 3401, Kindle.

23. King, *Trumpet of Conscience*, 62. Besides expanding his concept of the "inner spiritual church," King's use of the phrase "freedom church" explicitly "recalls the history of abolition and the role of religion and religious leadership in that revolutionary movement." Wessel-McCoy, "'Freedom Church of the Poor,'" 232.

a little bit, I'm going that way . . . If it means dying for them, I'm going that way.[24]

The inner church, then, is not a mystical association of initiates, invisible secret chiefs, or unknown superiors living in a hidden realm—it is the freedom church of the poor, led by the poor and dispossessed themselves to overturn the unjust and fallen structures of human society, and to bring the earthly city under the reign of the commonweal, the sphere of Christ the liberator.[25] Following the Hermetic maxim of "as above, so below," this irruption of the poor in history mirrors the movements of heaven: the freedom church of the poor, as the inner spiritual church founded on "the first day of the world's creation,"[26] is always moving the world closer to God's intention for it in the One Idea. The freedom church of the poor, the true *ekklesia*, is an "abbreviated image" of the Last Judgment, as the Christian theosopher Louis Claude de Saint-Martin, a contemporary of Eckartshausen, once said of the French Revolution: "Do not believe that our Revolution is an indifferent thing upon the earth . . . it is a miniature of the Last Judgment, with all its features."[27]

Resurrection City Knights

The allusion to the French Revolution brings up the specter of revolutionary violence, even though Dr. King was resolutely nonviolent. Those who are a part of contemporary movements for justice and equality can be understandably wary of military imagery, martial metaphors, and the language of warfare. After all, the beginning of the transition of Dr. King from civil rights to human rights is often ascribed to his sermon, "A Time to Break

24. Cited in Harding, *Martin Luther King*, 60.
25. Tiphareth, the sphere of the Son and of the Messiah. See chapter 2 of this book.
26. Von Eckartshausen, *Cloud upon the Sanctuary*, 33.
27. de Saint-Martin, *Theosophic Correspondence*, letter lxxii, 226. See Bates, "Mystery of Truth," 651–52.

Silence—Beyond Vietnam," given at New York City's Riverside Church in April 1967.[28] In this sermon, the first in which King publicly opposed President Johnson's war policy, King identified "the giant triplets of racism, extreme materialism, and militarism"[29] as interlinked—one could not be defeated without facing and defeating the other two. If King identified militarism in this way, as part of the "triple evils" along with racism and poverty, it would seem we can't utilize military imagery without damaging the necessarily intersectional nature of the justice movement, and without doing violence to King's commitment to nonviolence.

Yet King himself famously utilized such imagery in many of his key descriptions of the "inner spiritual church, the church within the church." In the 1967 Massey Lectures, King's first major articulation of the call for the Poor People's Campaign to confront those "giant triplets" of evil which he diagnosed in "A Time to Break Silence," King described the Poor People's Campaign using a combination of religious, political, *and* military imagery:

> The only real revolutionary, people say, is a man who has nothing to lose. There are millions of poor people in this country who have very little, or even nothing, to lose. If they can be helped to take action together, they will do so with a freedom and a power that will be a new and unsettling force in our complacent national life. Beginning in the New Year, we will be recruiting three thousand of the poorest citizens from ten different urban and rural areas to initiate and lead a sustained, massive, direct-action movement in Washington. Those who choose to join this initial three thousand, this nonviolent army, this "freedom church" of the poor, will work with us for three months to develop nonviolent action skills. Then we will move on Washington . . .[30]

The matrix of images King uses here to describe the call for the Poor People's Campaign displays his skill as a master orator.

28. See Wessel-McCoy, "Fifty Years Since 'Beyond Vietnam.'"
29. Wessel-McCoy, "Fifty Years Since 'Beyond Vietnam,'" para. 10.
30. King, *Trumpet of Conscience*, 62.

They require some unpacking to understand just what he is referring to and what the inspiration behind his images might be, especially the paradoxical image of a "nonviolent army."

In the recent call to build a new Poor People's Campaign, we frequently reference the notion of the poor and dispossessed as "a new and unsettling force."[31] Just as often, we refer to the force that must develop out of the leadership and unity of the poor as the freedom church of the poor. These images further establish that King's earlier identification of an "inner spiritual church, the church within the church" as the "hope of the world" had evolved by 1967 to locate this inner church in the potential of the organized poor to become a "new and unsettling force in our complacent national life"—as we have seen, the inner church *is* the freedom church of the poor.[32]

King's citing of "this initial three thousand" as comprising the freedom church of the poor is also theologically significant. The number 3,000 directly references the 3,000 souls who were saved at Pentecost in the Book of Acts.[33] King himself made this connection in his speech to the Southern Christian Leadership Conference (SCLC) staff during a retreat at Ebenezer Baptist Church on January 17, 1968:

> [Jesus called] a cursing sailor by the name of Peter. And old Peter vacillated. One day Jesus looked at him and said, in substance, "You are Simon now. Which meant

---

31. See the website of the Poor People's Campaign: A National Call for Moral Revival at http://poorpeoplescampaign.org.

32. Cf. Wessel-McCoy, "'Freedom Church of the Poor,'" 294: "When King asked from the Birmingham jail, 'Is organized religion too inextricably bound to the status quo to save our nation and the world?,' he found that indeed, though individual clergy would be leaven in the freedom struggles, it was ultimately 'the church within the church,' that would be 'the true ekklesia and the hope of the world.' And as the victories and defeats of the Civil Rights Movement gave way to his call for a human rights movement, King saw potential for a 'freedom church of the poor' as the hope of the world, theologically and politically."

33. Wessel-McCoy, "'Freedom Church of the Poor,'" 238: "King compares the 3,000 souls saved at Pentecost (Acts 2:41) to the 3,000 poor people they planned to bring to Washington D.C. for the Resurrection City occupation."

that you are sand, but I'm expecting you to be like a rock." And it was that pull of expectation that caused Peter, on the day of Pentecost to go out fired up with that something he got from Jesus, and he preached until three thousand souls were converted. Aren't we talking about three thousand? I'm expecting you to be like a rock. Now, we can do that, if we are fired up ourselves.[34]

The image of the "initial three thousand," then, explicitly describes the freedom church of the poor as emerging from a movement of the Holy Spirit; a contemporary Pentecost moment that would be facilitated by the leadership of the "church within the church" if they themselves were "fired up" by the Holy Spirit as was the apostle Peter.

In our current era, the Rev. Dr. William J. Barber II often utilizes similar imagery in his call for a "moral revival" in our still-complacent national life, a call that requires what he describes as "a political Pentecost in America today."[35] Not coincidentally, Rev. Barber serves as the co-chair of the new Poor People's Campaign.[36]

In what way, however, does the freedom church of the poor, the "initial three thousand" called into action by the Holy Spirit, resemble a "nonviolent army," and why would Dr. King resort to using such a martial metaphor? King's dedication to the spirituality and political practice of Gandhian nonviolence is well documented, and even in this section of the Massey Lectures he describes how the initial 3,000 would work with the SCLC for three months "to develop nonviolent action skills." Why, then, use the image of an army to describe this nonviolent "unsettling force?"

In linking the Holy Spirit-inspired unsettling force that would soon "move on Washington" with the image of an army, King implicitly invokes the image of other "armies" converging to wage a holy war on a major capital city. The implicit reference here

---

34. King, "See you in Washington (January 1968)," 10, cited in Wessel-McCoy, "'Freedom Church of the Poor,'" 238–39.

35. Barber, "HKonJ Seminar," cited in Wessel-McCoy, "'Freedom Church of the Poor,'" 3.

36. Kairos Center, "Breaking News!"

is probably to the Bonus Army of 1932, a comparison made both by the SCLC in their planning for the Poor People's Campaign and by the FBI in their internal discussions about the upcoming campaign.[37] As Colleen Wessel-McCoy describes it, the Bonus Army was a movement of poor veterans and their families to build

> a multiracial, unsegregated encampment in Anacostia in the spring and summer of 1932, demanding the early payment of earned service "adjusted compensation" that had been granted in the form of bonds that wouldn't mature until 1945.[38]

They called their encampment Hooverville "after then President Hoover, who ordered their removal on July 28, 1932 by a military force"[39]; the construction of a second encampment in May 1933 in Virginia during the Roosevelt administration resulted in gaining "the early full redemption in 1936, although only over Roosevelt's presidential veto."[40]

Yet Dr. King's linkage of the "nonviolent army of the poor" to the movement of the Holy Spirit during Pentecost inadvertently invites another historical comparison, and perhaps a less complimentary one—the medieval Crusades. During this much-maligned historical period, the Christian church of the Middle Ages summoned an army of crusaders to converge upon the Holy Land to divest the city of Jerusalem from Muslim control. The Crusades, especially the First Crusade of 1095, were preached to believers as holy movements led by God for the sake of justice and the freedom of Christian pilgrims—a kind of medieval "freedom church," but a decidedly violent one.

---

37. Wessel-McCoy, "'Freedom Church of the Poor,'" 188: "Shortly after learning of SCLC's encampment plans, the Johnson administration reached to the history and lessons of the Bonus Army, an occupation by former WWI veterans and their families during the Great Depression. This precedent was on the minds of the SCLC as well, a parallel pointed out to them by King advisor Stan Levinson."
38. Ibid., 189.
39. Ibid., 189.
40. Ibid., 189.

Indeed, the earliest expression of the crusading instinct was the launch of the "People's Crusade," also known as the "Peasant's Crusade" or the "Poor People's Crusade" in early 1096.[41] Rather than wait for the official launch of the First Crusade in August 1096, a motley band of peasants, poor people, and some minor nobles and knights decided to set off early for the Holy Land under the apocalyptic leadership of a monk known as Peter the Hermit—to disastrous results, both for the crusaders themselves and for the Jews of Eastern Europe.

Yet without wanting to approve of such a bloody venture, it must be said that the People's Crusade—as well as the Crusades as a whole—reflected the spiritual and material yearning of the medieval populace, including a large number of poor people to whom crusading in a foreign land under the banner of Christ seemed preferable to continuing to eke out an existence in the feudal social structure of medieval Europe. At the very least, the Poor People's Crusade has suffered from easy condemnation and a dearth of critical analysis that it shares with other poor people's movements throughout history, including the Bonus Army and the 1968 Poor People's Campaign.[42]

The Knights Templar, also known as the Order of Solomon's Temple or, especially evocative for our purposes here, the Poor Fellow-Soldiers of Christ, was formed in 1139 in the context of the Crusades. After the First Crusade recovered Jerusalem for Christendom, many Christians made pilgrimages to the Holy Land, including thousands of Western Europe's poor. Many of these pilgrims were killed along the way by bandits or highwaymen, resulting in the establishment of numerous knightly orders ideally dedicated to practicing the Christian theological virtues of faith, hope, and charity, and to the protection of the poorest pilgrims.

---

41. In fact, a Google search for the "Poor People's Crusade" or the "People's Crusade" returns a mix of results, half of them related to Martin Luther King Jr.'s 1968 Poor People's Campaign and half related to the actual medieval People's Crusade.

42. Duncalf, "Peasants' Crusade," 440: "The Peasants' Crusade of 1096 has been too generally regarded as a disorderly movement of misguided and unprepared rustics. The name suggests all this."

The most prominent of these was the Poor Fellow-Soldiers of Christ, better known as the Order of the Knights Templar, about which a great deal of nonsense has been written from the time of its persecution and dissolution in the fourteenth century all the way to the popular culture of today (see, to use the most prominent contemporary example, *The Da Vinci Code*).

But the serious use of the image and spirituality of the Knights Templar and other chivalric orders began much earlier than today's potboiler religious fiction. In the eighteenth century, a vogue for the chivalry of the medieval knightly orders began within the shadowy world of European Freemasonry. These secret societies spiritualized the knightly orders and utilized their symbolism to encode a system of mystical attainment merged with a system of Christian moral teaching.[43] Of course, the medieval orders were already both spiritual *and* martial, functioning as they did as lay spiritual orders dedicated to the sanctification of everyday life for the laity. The esoteric orders of the eighteenth century only built upon this spirituality to creatively combine the already existing Freemasonic symbolism with the symbolism of the knightly orders. The result of this process was the creation of an esoteric version of the spiritual or mystic chivalry of the Middle Ages, a nonviolent, inner spiritual church consisting of the Christian knightly orders of continental Freemasonry.

The parallel between the eighteenth-century appropriation of the martial chivalry of medieval knighthood for the mystic chivalry of the esoteric orders, and the appropriation of American military concepts for the nonviolent army of the Poor People's Campaign, extends beyond the level of imagery to the levels of spirituality and theology. According to A. E. Waite, the final Grade in the early Chapter of Clermont system of Freemasonry—a semi-mythical system of high degree French Masonry active between 1756 and 1763, which served as a prototype of Baron Von Hund's creation of the earliest Templar degrees in his Rite of Strict Observance—was the "Grade of Sublime Knight of God and of his Temple." The symbolism imparted in this degree related to

---

43. See Versluis, *Wisdom's Children*, chapter 20: "Theosophy and Chivalry."

the Holy City, the New Jerusalem, with its twelve gates, as a tabernacle of God with men. The Candidate is represented therefore as seeking the light of glory and a perfect recompense, while that which he is promised is an end of toils and trials. He is obligated as at the gates of the City and is promised the Grand Secret of those who abide therein. The City is—spiritually speaking—in the world to come, and the reward of chivalry is there; but there is a reward also on earth within the bonds of the Order, because this is said to be divine and possessed of the treasures of wisdom.[44]

This reward, the grand secret of the Templars perpetuated (according to the legend of this degree) under the guise of Masonry after their destruction as an exoteric institution in 1312, was, according to Waite, the formula of the Philosopher's Stone—that precious stone that can transmute base metals into gold, and, in the cosmic sense, transmute the material world into the resurrection body, the spiritual body St. Paul speaks of in 1 Corinthians.[45] For the mystical alchemists seeking the Philosopher's Stone were not mere chemists trying to create riches out of dross—they were spiritual seekers who attempted to find a path to *theosis* or divinization. As W. B. Yeats wrote,

> their doctrine was no merely chemical phantasy, but a philosophy they applied to the world, to the elements and to man himself; and . . . they sought to fashion gold out of common metals merely as part of a universal transmutation of all things into some divine and imperishable substance.[46]

The *telos* of mystic chivalry is thus the transmutation of all things—cosmic *theosis*—and the fullness of this goal is to be found in the Holy City of the New Jerusalem, the biblical symbol

---

44. Waite, "Templar Orders in Freemasonry," location 1904 of 2,116, Kindle.

45. 1 Cor 15:44: "It is sown a physical body, it is raised a spiritual body. If there is a physical body, there is also a spiritual body" (NRSV).

46. Yeats, "Rosa Alchemica," para. 2.

of creation being set to rights with the final advent of God's eschatological kingdom. This includes the eschatological regeneration of human society, typified in the Book of Revelation's account of the New Jerusalem by the image of the Tree of Life, whose leaves "are for the healing of the nations."[47]

It must be remembered, however, that in Waite's esoteric account of the final grade of the early Templar rite, the postulant "is obligated as at the gates of the City," in which the fullness of his reward resides; he does not enter the Holy City itself, for it is—"spiritually speaking—in the world to come." The Templar might receive the knowledge of the Philosopher's Stone, or the path to *theosis*, in this life, but complete cosmic transmutation will have to await the eschaton or the world to come. Mystic chivalry's goal is thus eschatological, but its struggle is this-worldly—the Christian knight does not enter the Holy City at the end of his quest in order to remove himself from the fallen world and its tribulations, but utilizes the heavenly wisdom gained "at the gates of the City" to participate in that "universal transmutation of all things" that Yeats describes so poetically.

In short, mystic chivalry is a form of social theology—a spirituality of world transformation and reformation. The step from here to Dr. King's neochivalric "nonviolent army of the poor" and its liberative crusade to alter the unjust social structures of our world is a simple one. While the world is still suffering from the chains of oppression, the freedom church of the poor must maintain an activist spirituality, like the Knights Templars of old. If the original Poor People's Campaign built a symbolic Resurrection City in the form of the campaign's encampment on the National Mall in Washington, D.C., the inner church seeks to build a Holy City, the New Jerusalem or the City of the Silver Star, as an eschatological reality. Rev. Ralph Abernathy, Dr. King's successor in the SCLC, reflected on Resurrection City in utopian terms:

47. Rev 22:1–2: "Then the angel showed me the river of the water of life, bright as crystal, flowing from the throne of God and of the Lamb through the middle of the street of the city. On either side of the river is the tree of life with its twelve kinds of fruit, producing its fruit each month; and the leaves of the tree are for the healing of the nations" (NRSV).

THE INNER CHURCH IS THE HOPE OF THE WORLD: CONSUMMATION

> We would set up a model for the rest of the nation to emulate. Everyone would live together in peace and mutual respect . . . we would have people of all races, ethnic backgrounds and religious beliefs. Since everyone would be poor, there would be no greed or envy . . . (A) City on the Hill, where we would live the Good Life as a witness to the entire nation.[48]

As Wessel-McCoy points out, for Abernathy to think of a physical encampment built in protest in swampy, rain-drenched Washington, D. C. in this way was only setting himself up for disappointment. Still, the eschatological image here is resonant with the symbolism of the New Jerusalem—the Holy City to which the esoteric Templars quested. And it is consonant with Dr. King's own image of the city that the "initial three thousand," the nonviolent army of the poor, would seek:

> By the thousands we will move. Many will wonder where we are coming from. Our only answer will be that we are coming up out of great trials and tribulation. Some of us will come from Mississippi, some of us will come from Cleveland. But we will all be coming from the same conditions. We will be seeking a city whose Builder and Maker is God, and if we will do this we will be able to turn this nation upside down and right side up. We may just be able to speed up the day when man everywhere will respect the dignity and worth of human personality and all men will be able to cry out that we are children of God made in His image. This will be a glorious day and that moment the morning stars will sing together and the son of God will shout for joy.[49]

The "morning stars will sing together and the son of God will shout for joy"[50]—an image of those saints in light, the secret chiefs of the Silver Star, and the Silver Star of Bethlehem around

---

48. Abernathy, *And the Walls Came Tumbling Down*, 502–3; cited in Wessel-McCoy, "'Freedom Church of the Poor,'" 117.

49. King Jr., "State of the Movement (November 1967)," 12; cited in Wessel-McCoy, "'Freedom Church of the Poor,'" 233.

50. Ibid., 233.

THE INNER CHURCH

which they pay homage, shouting for joy at the creation of the true Resurrection City, the eschatological community of the New Jerusalem.

As we have seen, the leaders of the poor and dispossessed—often unknown in a society that ignores and marginalizes them—are the "unknown cadre" of the freedom church of the poor. Made up of those hidden saints "who have most capacity for light," the inner church is the assembly of the elect in the world but not of the world, a new and unsettling force "who have very little, or even nothing, to lose," those leaders of the poor and dispossessed who have become free from the distorted moral narrative of our fallen society.[51] The inner church is the freedom church of the poor, the true *ekklesia* of those who have made themselves pure enough to acts as prisms for the light of God, as real manifestations in our world of the One Idea of God for God's creation—a world of abundance, without systemic racism, poverty, and militarism, the moral obscenities that Dr. King organized against.

The inner church, the freedom church of the poor, is the hope of the world. And until the world conforms to God's One Idea, to which all the saints in light and all the unknown superiors and all the secret chiefs of the Silver Star are guiding us, the inner church must also be on a nonviolent crusade to alter the unjust social structures of our society. In other words, the freedom church of the poor must also be the nonviolent army of the poor, the spiritual templars who crusade toward "a city whose Builder and Maker is God," what we know as the City of the Silver Star. In our final chapter, we will turn to this image of the Holy City, toward which we, too, have been questing.

---

51. Eckartshausen, *Cloud upon the Sanctuary*, 34; King, *Trumpet of Conscience*, 62.

VI

City of the Silver Star

> We will be seeking a city whose Builder and Maker is God...
>
> —Rev. Dr. Martin Luther King Jr.[1]

Toward a New Humanity

THE SPIRITUAL CHIVALRY OF Western Esotericism brings us to the gates of the Holy City—empowering us as nonviolent spiritual knights acting as guardians of the New Jerusalem that, as the consummation of the spiritual and political liberation wrought by Jesus Christ, is preparing to descend to Earth from the kingdom of heaven.[2] According to the insights of liberation theologians like Juan Luis Segundo, human effort is required to prepare the way for this Holy City, this City of the Silver Star to which we have been guided by the inner church that seeks the liberation of the cosmos by conforming it to the likeness of the One Idea of God, the Logos that is identified with Christ Jesus in the Christian tradition. Drawing on Teilhard de Chardin, Segundo writes, "the effort to build a better world is nothing else in fact than the effort of Christification"—the progressive transfiguration of the cosmos into the Christ, into the One Idea—"just as the effort of the People of Israel was a slow and progressive effort making possible the incarnation of the Word, so the effort that is

---

1. King, "State of the Movement (November 1967)," 12; cited in Wessel-McCoy, "'Freedom Church of the Poor,'" 233.
2. Rev 21:2.

required for the progress of the cosmos is nurturing the recapitulation of all things in Christ."[3]

Humanity alone cannot bring about the New Jerusalem—God must crown our human project with God's grace. As the Neophyte Ceremony of the Golden Dawn states,

> Remember that God alone is our light and the bestower of perfect wisdom, and that no mortal power can do more than bring you to the pathway of that wisdom, which He could, if it so pleased Him, put into the heart of a child.[4]

But according to both liberation theologians like Segundo and the occultists of the Golden Dawn, we must make our own way to the "pathway of that wisdom."[5] According to Segundo, God cannot redeem what humanity does not first build using our own efforts—we must make our way to the gates of the Holy City if God is to infuse our efforts with God's grace.

How can we assist the liberating God in God's project of building the City of the Silver Star, with the guidance of that unknown cadre in light that have already conformed themselves to God's One Idea for the cosmos? How do our political and social movements contribute to such a project? Much like Edward Schillebeeckx's future *humanum,* which we can only catch glimpses of in our struggles against injustice, Segundo saw the furtherance of God's project in terms of the creation of a new humanity, drawing on Teilhard de Chardin's evolutionary parable of the humanity of our era finally becoming the pilot of the ship of the cosmos.[6] Segundo's project of building the new humanity is reminiscent of the oath of an Adeptus Minor in the Golden Dawn: "I pledge myself to hereby give myself to the great Work, which is so to exalt my lower nature that I may at length become more than human, and thus gradually raise and unite myself to my Higher and Divine

---

3. Segundo, *Grace and the Human Condition*, 84.
4. Regardie, *Golden Dawn,* 130.
5. Ibid., 130.
6. Segundo, *Community Called Church*, 121.

Genius"—which, as we have seen, can be expanded from an individualistic drive to exalt *oneself* into a communitarian project of exalting *humanity*, or even the whole cosmos.[7]

In concrete terms, to build this new humanity, to reach the *humanum*, requires strengthening our commitment to ending the oppressions that prevent humanity from taking this evolutionary step, from becoming conscious and reflective pilots of the ship of the cosmos rather than mere passengers (or, worse, prisoners). The National Union of the Homeless mission statement, released in May, 1988, put it this way: "We pledge to deepen our personal commitment to end all forms of exploitation, racism, sexism, and abuse. True solidarity demands that we create not only the new society, but also the new human being."[8] The NUH aimed to accomplish this through a "sustained struggle" and "revolutionary perseverance"—through building a movement committed to "economic justice, human rights, and full liberation."[9] To reach the city whose "Builder and Maker is God," and to arrive at that moment when "the morning stars will sing together and the son of God will shout for joy"—a perfect image of the inner church and the One Idea of God in the biblical language of Dr. King—we must not only seek a new society through our movement building and our spiritual work, but also a new humanity. In this chapter we will examine some contemporary social and political movements that might help us to discover this future-oriented new humanity—the citizens of the City of the Silver Star—and some esoteric movements that might spiritually compliment such a goal.

---

7. Regardie, *Golden Dawn*, 230.

8. National Union of the Homeless mission statement, May 1988, *The National Union of the Homeless: A Brief History*. The NUH was part of an ecology of organizations related to the welfare rights movement, the Kensington Welfare Rights Union, and eventually to the Kairos Center and the new Poor People's Campaign of 2017–18.

9. Ibid.

Accelerating to the Future

We live in an era of great plenty, in the midst of unprecedented abundance. Yet we also live in a time of artificial scarcity—calls for austerity, rationalistic excuses for massive economic inequality, and attacks on the poor in the name of a death-dealing morality masquerading as level-headed budgetary concern. On the left and right, a fatalistic obsession with the temporary autonomous zone—brief moments supposedly free from the control of restrictive and rapacious neoliberal capitalism—replace speculative visions of a better future that once drove both the political imaginaries of social movements, and the utopian aspirations of Western esotericists. In the memorable phrase of Nick Srnicek, Alex Williams, and Armen Avanessian, "the future has been cancelled."[10]

Yet some new political formations are fighting back against this tendency in contemporary politics. The obscenity of poverty in an era of plenty is one of the primary arguments behind the call for a new Poor People's Campaign, the work of the Kairos Center, Repairers of the Breach, and many other movement organizations to complete the unfinished work of Dr. King's original Poor People's Campaign of 1968. King knew then that abundance should be the right of every human being. At Frogmore, South Carolina, on November 14, 1966, King said,

> God has left enough (and to spare) in this world for all of his children to have the basic necessities of life, and God never intended for some of his children to live in inordinate superfluous wealth while others live in abject, deadening poverty. And somehow I believe that God made it all . . . I believe firmly that the earth is the Lord's and the fullness thereof. I don't think it belongs to Mr. Rockefeller. I don't think it belongs to Mr. Ford. I think the earth is the Lord's, and since we didn't make these things by ourselves, we must share them with each other. And I think this is the only way we are going to solve

---

10. Avanessian et al., "#Accelerationism: Remembering the Future," para. 1.

the basic problems and the restructuring of our society, which I think is so desperately needed.[11]

Yet fifty years after Dr. King spoke these words, we still live in a society based on artificial scarcity, a world of growing economic inequality, and rising global poverty. This is why we need a new moral movement to end poverty, backed by the kind of liberative theology and spirituality suggested by Dr. King, and led by the poor and dispossessed themselves:

> In our times this liberative spirituality is distinguished by the demand it makes for the "right to not be poor." Today we have the unprecedented capacity to provide every human being with enough to not only survive but to thrive. And yet life is devalued and discarded on a grand scale. By rejecting this world where great wealth and productivity exists alongside tremendous human neglect, the leaders and communities of struggle across this nation and world are showing all of us the possibility of a new way of being. It will be a world where all life is valued and the right to not be poor is guaranteed for everyone.
>
> The driving force of this liberative spirituality today is its orientation around the leadership of the poor. This does not mean that being poor necessarily makes one a great leader. Those who are dispossessed and made poor by this system (the vast majority) are leaders in the sense that their experience and voice indict our current system's devaluation of life. Their struggles, therefore, uphold the value of all life, and help awaken all people—rich or poor—to the lies of this system and its immoral theology.[12]

There is much in common between the politics of abundance, the liberative theology and spirituality of the poor, and Srnicek and Williams's vision of a "left accelerationism"—a political tendency rooted in the belief that the future must be newly constructed by a reinvigorated left unafraid of embracing contemporary

11. Kairos Center, "Dr. King's Speech," para. 14.
12. Barnes and Gupta Barnes, "America, You Must be Born Again!," paras. 22–23.

technology and productive forces. As Srnicek and Williams write in their "Manifesto for an Accelerationist Politics,"

> We need to revive the argument that was traditionally made for post-capitalism: not only is capitalism an unjust and perverted system, but it is also a system that holds back progress. Our technological development is being suppressed by capitalism, as much as it has been unleashed. Accelerationism is the basic belief that these capacities can and should be let loose by moving beyond the limitations imposed by capitalist society.[13]

The left accelerationists contrast the "folk politics of localism, direct action, and relentless horizontalism" with what they call "an accelerationist politics at ease with a modernity of abstraction, complexity, globality, and technology."[14] While the former focuses its attention on establishing temporary autonomous zones and on "registering discontent" rather than building the power necessary to truly restructure society, the latter "seeks to preserve the gains of late capitalism while going further than its value system, governance structures, and mass pathologies will allow."[15]

What truly distinguishes left accelerationism from the anarchist tendencies recently dominating popular leftist movements is the former's emphasis on unleashing the "latent productive forces" of modern technology:

> Accelerationists want to unleash latent productive forces. In this project, the material platform of neoliberalism does not need to be destroyed. It needs to be repurposed towards common ends. The existing infrastructure is not a capitalist stage to be smashed, but a springboard to launch towards post-capitalism.[16]

Srnicek and Williams "want to accelerate the process of technological evolution." But this is not the same as techno-utopianism

---

13. Srnicek and Williams, "#Accelerate Manifesto," para. 22.
14. Ibid., 3.1.
15. Ibid., 3.1.
16. Ibid., 3.5.

or a new post-capitalist technocracy. As the #Accelerate Manifesto states,

> Never believe that technology will be sufficient to save us. Necessary, yes, but never sufficient without sociopolitical action. Technology and the social are intimately bound up with one another, and changes in either potentiate and reinforce changes in the other. Whereas the techno-utopians argue for acceleration on the basis that it will automatically overcome social conflict, our position is that technology should be accelerated precisely because it is needed in order to win social conflicts.[17]

The left accelerationists (as distinguished from the pro-capitalist accelerationism of Nick Land and the alt-right, and the dystopian libertarianism so popular today in Silicon Valley) thus argue for an acceleration with direction, with a *telos*—not a mad dash to the future, but a planned one. This means bypassing the fetishizing of process and horizontalism on the contemporary left:

> The overwhelming privileging of democracy-as-process needs to be left behind. The fetishisation of openness, horizontality, and inclusion of much of today's "radical" left set the stage for ineffectiveness. Secrecy, verticality, and exclusion all have their place as well in effective political action (though not, of course, an exclusive one).[18]

The manifesto avoids prescribing any single organization as the solution to the problems it raises—in fact, it suggests that no particular organization could embody all the vectors of what is needed to actualize an accelerationist politics. Instead, what is needed "is an ecology of organisations, a pluralism of forces, resonating and feeding back on their comparative strengths."[19]

In terms of concrete movement politics, such a vision of an "ecology of organizations" is a good description of the movement we are building with the new Poor People's Campaign, which

---

17. Ibid., 3.7.
18. Ibid., 3.13.
19. Ibid., 3.15.

also fulfills the demand of the manifesto to "reconstitute various forms of class power."[20] The notion of the unity and leadership of the poor and dispossessed as articulated by the Kairos Center is a reconstitution of class that, in the words of the manifesto, moves "beyond the notion that an organically generated global proletariat already exists." Instead, our work to build the movement to end poverty attempts "to knit together a disparate array of partial proletarian identities, often embodied in post-Fordist forms of precarious labour," such as the homeless, those living in tent cities, those involved in underground economies, the postindustrial unemployed and underemployed, and indebted students and academics.[21]

Building Universality from Below

There are many similarities between the growing movement to end poverty and the thinking of the left accelerationists. And the accelerationist drive to reach the future could help reinstate some of the utopianism we've found in both the Western esoteric tradition and in the theologies of liberation. Yet some critiques of the left accelerationist position might be fruitful to consider both in terms of the growing movement of the poor and dispossessed and the quest to discover a new humanity that we described above in the work of Segundo, the Golden Dawn tradition, and others.

Though he sees value in its innovative approach to left politics, Alexander R. Galloway criticizes left accelerationism as a kind of "brometheanism"—a telling insult that suggests that left accelerationists tend to be both male, straight, and white, and to be futurists obsessed with the utopian possibilities of modern technology.[22] A bromethean is thus a kind of millennial cross between the Silicon Valley tech bro and the bros involved with the most polemical forms of communist vanguardism—all reworked and

---

20. Ibid., 3.18.
21. Ibid., 3.18.
22. Galloway, "Brometheanism."

polished for guys who grew up watching Robert Downey, Jr. in *Iron Man*. Instead, Galloway suggests that a much better use of the accelerationist current on the left is the Xenofeminist Manifesto, produced by the avant-garde feminist collective Laboria Cuboniks. Xenofeminism, Galloway explains, is more concerned with building a kind of "universalism from below" rather than arguing for technological utopianism from the high vantage point of defaulted cis-heteronormative white maleness.[23]

Entitled *Xenofeminism: A Politics for Alienation*, the Xenofeminist Manifesto is more alien, more future-oriented, and more universalist than the "Manifesto for an Accelerationist Politics":

> Ours is a world in vertigo. It is a world that swarms with technological mediation, interlacing our daily lives with abstraction, virtuality, and complexity. XF [Xenofeminism] constructs a feminism adapted to these realities: a feminism of unprecedented cunning, scale, and vision; a future in which the realization of gender justice and feminist emancipation contribute to a universalist politics assembled from the needs of every human, cutting across race, ability, economic standing, and geographical position.[24]

While the left accelerationists suggest that a successful movement for radical social change might need to leave behind the modern left's emphasis on inclusion and horizontality, the Xenofeminist Manifesto explodes the traditional inclusivism and horizontalism of the left in its attempt to forge a true universalism, including everyone and everything—regardless of gender (or lack thereof), race, or sexuality. This is not done from above, in the illusory and oppressive manner of the Enlightenment notion of the white, cis-heteronormative, European male as the default human subject, who alone can survey the world in a rational and neutrally objective way. Instead, the xenofeminists argue for a universality from below, a grassroots universalism built laterally (horizontally?) across traditional lines of division:

23. Ibid., para. 28.
24. Laboria Cuboniks, *Xenofeminism*, 0x00.

Xenofeminism understands that the viability of emancipatory abolitionist projects—the abolition of class, gender, and race—hinges on a profound reworking of the universal. The universal must be grasped as generic, which is to say, intersectional. Intersectionality is not the morcellation of collectives into a static fuzz of cross-referenced identities, but a political orientation that slices through every particular, refusing the crass pigeonholing of bodies. This is not a universal that can be imposed from above, but built from the bottom up—or, better, laterally, opening new lines of transit across an uneven landscape. This non-absolute, generic universality must guard against the facile tendency of conflation with bloated, unmarked particulars—namely Eurocentric universalism—whereby the male is mistaken for the sexless, the white for raceless, the cis for the real, and so on.[25]

The xenofeminists take to heart the powerful postmodern critique of Enlightenment reason and objectivity, but without giving up on the modernist dream of a true universal subject—especially in the service of human rights. The Xenofeminist Manifesto thus articulates a politics for the era after postmodernism, a queerer, more gender-fluid, and more alien politics than the stark modernism of the traditional left, but also a politics that is still dedicated to the idea of universal human rights and organized movement building:

> From the postmoderns, we have learnt to burn the facades of the false universal . . . from the moderns, we have learnt to sift new universals from the ashes of the false. Xenofeminism seeks to construct a coalitional politics, a politics without the infection of purity. Wielding the universal requires thoughtful qualification and precise self-reflection so as to become a ready-to-hand tool for multiple political bodies and something that can be appropriated against the numerous oppressions that transect with gender and sexuality. The universal is no blueprint, and rather than dictate its uses in advance, we propose XF as a platform. The very process of

25. Ibid., 0x0F.

construction is therefore understood to be a negentropic, iterative, and continual refashioning. Xenofeminism seeks to be a mutable architecture that, like open source software, remains available for perpetual modification and enhancement following the navigational impulse of militant ethical reasoning.[26]

Many of the movements that have joined up with the new Poor People's Campaign and the work to spark a broad moral movement to end poverty, racism, militarism, and ecological devastation today already participate in this grassroots version of the human rights imperative—human rights in the service of the struggles of the bottom, rather than rights as assigned from the top down by governments and world authorities like the United Nations. As Larry Cox, co-director of the Kairos Center and former executive director of Amnesty International, often notes about the origin of human rights,

> That governments were not the source of the power of human rights should not be a surprise. For the foundational idea of human rights is that they are *not* the creation of governments. They are not created *at all* but discovered, usually through the fight against their violation. As is often proclaimed but less often seriously examined, human rights are inherent in every human being at birth. All governments can do is formulate, recognize, and respect them. They can respond and add to their power but they cannot create them.[27]

The xenofeminist emphases on alienation, lateral movement-building, and artifice (which goes far beyond the accelerationist interest in utopian technicity and lands squarely in the queerer traditions of glam, pulp sci-fi, and literary decadence) don't sound immediately as harmonious with the grassroots work of building a social movement as do the radical yet recognizable emphases of the left accelerationists. But the key point—the drive to build a universality from below in the support of grassroots human rights

26. Ibid., 0x10.
27. Cox, "Power of Religion," para. 22.

that truly represents the interests of the poor and dispossessed, especially across traditional lines of division such as race, geography, gender, and sexuality—does deeply align the work of growing social movements with the xenofeminist political current.

Rev. Dr. William J. Barber II, the co-chair of the recent Poor People's Campaign, often frames the leadership of the poor and dispossessed in terms of "the rejected"—the rejected must lead the revival, according to Barber:

> In America and in the world, the rejected are gonna lead the revival. I need to know, are there any folk that know what it's like to be rejected? But in your rejection, God has revived you and reconciled you and redeemed you and there is a rejoicing that only the rejected can do. I wonder is there is a rejection praise in here? They said I'd never make it. They said I wouldn't be nobody. They said I was too gay, too radical, too lesbian, too poor, but look at what the Lord has done! The stone that the builders rejected has become the chief cornerstone! Somebody just ought to stop talking and start praising it! And give him glory! And say neighbor, watch a rejected person rejoice![28]

The alienated subjects of the Xenofeminist Manifesto are surely a part of the rejected of American society, even a part of the rejected of the liberal and progressive left. All of these rejected folks—the ones who were called too queer, too disabled, too poor to be a part of past movements—must share in the leadership and unity of any growing social movement, if it is going to build a true universality from below, a truly new humanity for a new society, rather than another iteration of "the given masked as critique."[29]

One reason why many segments of that alienated class called "the rejected" might not have been drawn into the efforts to build a broad social movement in the United States thus far is that the religious and spiritual keynotes of movements like the Poor People's Campaign and the moral movement, though radical and

---

28. Kairos Center, "Rejected Will Lead the Revival," para. 1.
29. Laboria Cuboniks, *Xenofeminism*, 0x00.

liberative, have still been very traditional. By and large, prayers before our events have been from representatives of the world religions, and largely from the Abrahamic religions. Frequently, though many young people (especially young queer people) in this country are very skeptical of organized religion and of professional clergypeople, these folks have still largely made up the spiritual reserves of our growing nonviolent army of the poor.

If this nonviolent army is really going to "break every chain," as we frequently sang at the end of each 2017 Mass Meeting of the Poor People's Campaign, then it will need to include representatives from religious cultures and currents that might be seen at first as more alien—or just plain *weirder*—than the usual progressive religious traditions that are already well-represented at our events and in our organizing. One example of these cultures, one that I'd wager has a great deal of crossover with people for whom the Xenofeminist Manifesto resonates deeply, is the world of occult spirituality—the rejected knowledge of Western esotericism for the rejected who make up the cornerstone of the growing moral movement.

In fact, examining esotericism in terms of popular movements for social justice is not so alien to the history of either esotericism or the history of popular movements. The universal human rights framework, especially as it is conceived of and utilized in the United States—based on the Declaration of Independence's statement that "We hold these truths to be self-evident, that all men are created equal, that they are endowed by their creator with certain unalienable Rights, that among these are life, liberty, and the pursuit of happiness"—was indirectly influenced by the participation of many of the American Founding Fathers and other eighteenth-century intellectuals in Freemasonry, which was in many ways an attempt to put the philosophy of the Enlightenment into experiential, symbolic practice.[30]

Additionally, African American Freemasonry—also known as Prince Hall Freemasonry—has had a noted role in the struggle of black Americans to achieve freedom, equality, and enfranchisement.

---

30. See Hackett, *That Religion*, 60.

In the 1960s, the SCLC headquarters was in the Prince Hall Masonic Temple in Atlanta, Georgia. According to the King Center, "many Prince Hall Masons were active in the civil rights movement."[31] Scholar Corey D. B. Walker has studied how black Freemasonry functioned as a laboratory of democracy in the early nineteenth century.[32] Walker argues that Prince Hall Freemasonry provides a lens for "understanding the distinctive ways African Americans have constructed a radically democratic political imaginary through racial solidarity and political nationalism," and examines the history of Prince Hall Freemasonry to revisit "the complex relationship between voluntary associations and democratic politics." For example, Walker locates some of the inspiration behind the early-nineteenth-century slave rebellion led by Virginia slave and blacksmith Gabriel Prosser in the complex symbolism of black Freemasonry.[33]

Radical Freemasonry and the Moral Movement

The connections between Freemasonry and the Radical Enlightenment ideas of the European revolutionary period, and between Prince Hall Masonry and movements for black liberation and civil rights in the United States, have been well established. But Masonry, of all the esoteric currents, might seem like the worst tradition upon which to try and build a universality from below—after all, "regular" Anglo-American Freemasonry (generally defined as Masonic bodies "in amity" with or recognized by the United Grand Lodge of England) only initiates men, and until the second half of the twentieth century, American lodges did not even recognize their African American brothers of the Prince Hall tradition.

31. The King Center, "Freemasons, Prince Hall Grand Lodge," para. 1.

32. Walker, *Noble Fight*.

33. In fact, there may be some direct influence of Prince Hall Masonry on the growing moral movement/Poor People's Campaign: A National Call for Moral Revival—as his biography from the NAACP explains, Rev. Dr. Barber himself is a Prince Hall Mason who has reached the 33rd degree of the Scottish Rite, the highest level in that body of American Masonry.

Furthermore, "regular" Masons must profess a belief in a higher power, and sometimes a belief in an afterlife. No organization or tradition that excludes over fifty percent of the population, that has such a painful history of white supremacy and segregation, and that excludes such a growing segment of the population of the modern world (atheists and agnostics), could ever be seen as a universal movement, no matter how lay it is in terms of its spirituality.

But the aims of Masonry, as defined in its eighteenth-century constitutions and in its ritual work, do suggest something more in line with the universal human rights vision of Rev. Barber's moral movement—and even with the xenofeminist vision of laterally cutting across all lines of division to create a truly universal movement from below. The traditional Masonic stricture against discussing politics and religion within the lodge—which seems on the face of it to be an impossible and ridiculous ideal considering the deep religious and political aspects of Masonic tradition and history—actually supports a kind of grassroots spirituality that is based on the lived experience of ritual work rather than a creedal assent to dogmatic or partisan belief systems. In this, the Masonic lodge resembles a mass meeting or direct action of the Poor People's Campaign—which, taking the lead of Rev. Barber's moral movement, rejects partisan political labels and dogmatic religious structures. Instead, the Poor People's Campaign is built up through the solidarity of the poor and dispossessed taking action together in the service of our deepest shared moral values, rather than any partisan political ideas or dogmatic theological concepts.[34]

Similarly, Masons are made Masons through engaging in the ritual work together—using the metaphor of building the Temple of Solomon, here allegorized into the building up of a Masonic lodge, the building up of one's moral character, and the moral perfecting of human society. Like the solidarity of the moral movement taking action in the streets, Masons build fraternity through the *work*.[35] And the radical Enlightenment roots of Freemasonry

---

34. For more on Rev. Barber's concept of the moral movement, see Barber and Wilson-Hartgrove, *Third Reconstruction*.

35. Reilly, "Freemasonry," para. 11.

suggest that the current rules against initiating women or people of different races or religious identities actually militates against the true potential and vision of the Masonic Brotherhood.

Two traditions of Masonry currently embrace this history, rather than rejecting it in favor of political and cultural conformity, as do the Anglo-American Grand Lodges: the French continental traditions of the Grand Orient of France—which removed the religious requirement for initiation in the second half of the nineteenth century (at which point the Anglo-American lodges stopped recognizing it as "regular") and began to initiate women in 2010—and the International Order of Freemasonry for Men and Women, Le Droit Humain—which was the first Masonic order to be truly international (it has lodges in over sixty countries), and, most importantly, to accept women as initiates. Both the Grand Orient of France and Le Droit Humain emphasize the radical, lay, secular spirituality of Freemasonry, and actively declare their support for human rights and progressive political causes.[36]

It is unlikely that we will see a sudden influx of young radicals into the lodges of Le Droit Humain, and perhaps equally unlikely that any Masonic lodges will actually endorse something like the Poor People's Campaign. But the Masonic ideal provides spiritual resources for a moral movement that aims to build a grassroots universality from below, a universal moral temple for the whole human race, a City of the Silver Star whose builder and Maker is God. And perhaps the values of the Poor People's Campaign could reinvigorate the aging and socially staid demographics of the Masonic lodges of the twenty-first century.

Coming from the Sphere of the Future

There is one important tradition that emerged out of the fringe Freemasonry of the esoteric circles of the late nineteenth century, and which has since influenced every significant movement in the world of occultism and esotericism in the twentieth and

---

36. For more on the tradition of Continental Freemasonry and Le Droit Humain in particular, see Lorente-Bull and Rees, *More Light*.

twenty-first centuries: the Hermetic Order of the Golden Dawn. This order, which organizes itself into lodges like the Masons, teaches esoteric philosophy, occultism, and the practice of ritual magic. Unlike regular Freemasonry, it initiates both men and women, and explicitly espouses a form of Hermetic religious philosophy, even though ritual work and lived experience is still the paramount landmark of the order. Without the Golden Dawn, no major current of twentieth-century esotericism would exist the way it does today—from Gerald Gardner's Wicca to Aleister Crowley's Thelema, from the Chaos Magic current of the 1980s to the fad for Tarot cards among millennials today (two of the most popular Tarot decks of the twentieth century, the Rider-Waite Tarot and the Thoth Tarot, were both created by members of the Golden Dawn).

The name of Aleister Crowley is indelibly associated in popular culture with the Golden Dawn, even though he was only a member of the order for about a year and a half and took the Golden Dawn system in radically different directions after the order's schisms at the turn of the century. Crowley's new religious movement, Thelema, draws heavily on Golden Dawn magic, as well as on yoga, Theravada Buddhism, and Crowley's own personal visions and idiosyncrasies. Thelema is primarily based on Crowley's revelation of *The Book of the Law* or *Liber AL vel Legis*, a transmitted text that Crowley received with the assistance of his wife, Rose, in Cairo in 1904. Crowley believed himself to be the prophet of the New Aeon of Horus, which replaces the former Aeon of Osiris, whose now outmoded formula of the dying and rising God was perhaps best expressed in organized Christianity and the story of the crucified and risen Christ. Crowley was deeply anti-Christian, yet also deeply influenced by Christian theology, as he was raised in a strict English Protestant community, the Plymouth Brethren. He was also deeply misogynistic, prone to aristocratic and protofascist fantasies, and a white supremacist—yet his movement has grown into a truly diverse and new religious tradition within Western esotericism.[37]

37. For a summary of Crowley's life, his involvement in the Golden Dawn,

Like its predecessor, the Golden Dawn, Crowley's Thelema has itself blossomed into a number of different currents, many of which are far more egalitarian, and potentially more radical, than Crowley himself. I would like to briefly describe one such current: the Maatian tradition of the Horus/Maat Lodge, a "virtual lodge" that has participants across the world and espouses a kind of queer futurism that shares some resemblances with the xenofeminist current.

Crowley's Aeonic philosophy, which posits that we live in spiritual eras with specific formulae and ritual expressions, has influenced the Aquarian age ideas of the 1960s and the new age spiritualities of the 1980s (not to mention the revival of Crowley's own Thelemic organizations during the broader occult revival of the 1970s). Unlike other expressions of Thelema, the Horus/Maat Lodge—founded by a group of young magicians and occultists on April 26, 1979 under the influence of the Thelemic magician Nema (Margaret Ingalls), and now a virtual lodge movement that exists primarily on the internet across geographical boundaries—argues that we live in the Aeon of a "double-current." In this formulation, both Crowley's Horus—the Crowned and Conquering Child—and the goddess Maat—an expression of the divine feminine whose Aeon is marked by the fulfillment of truth and justice, of universal human rights, and the embrace of more fluid sexual, gender, and political identities—are active at the same time, an impossibility according to Thelemic orthodoxy.[38] Don Karr cites a passage explaining the meaning of the "double-current" from the website of occultist and artist Orryelle Defenestrate-Bascule:

> In 1974 Priestess Nema received a transmission from Maat, *Liber Pennae Praenumbra,* during a timetravel working within the Thelemic tradition established by Crowley. Her angle on the "double current" of Horus and Maat is that the Maat current is coming backwards

and the development of Thelema as a religious movement, see Kaczynski, *Perdurabo*.

38. Horus/Maat Lodge F.A.Q., cited in Karr, *Approaching the Kabbalah of Maat*, 70.

from a future aeon . . . when time is perceived differently, manifesting now through those open enough to receive the information, the "mutants" who are the avatars of the coming race of "homo veritas." The aim of Maat Magick now is primarily to awaken the collective unconscious of humanity, linking us all in universal empathy.[39]

The Aeon of Maat comes to use from the future, while the Aeon of Horus, through warlike "force and fire," establishes itself by the ever-accelerating present. The point at which these two Aeons meet is our eschatological *kairos* moment, a moment in which we can catch a glimpse of the future shape of the human being—in the "mutants" who are the avatars of "the coming race of 'homo veritas.'"[40]

This coming race, the "homo veritas," is identified in the work of Nema and the Horus/Maat Lodge with the being called "N'Aton," who first manifested during a group magical working in 1973.[41] N'Aton is the collective humanity of the future, the shared superconciousness who "'sleeps' in all—or *most*—of us and is gradually waking up. 'He/she/we' is our future selves, the future of our species, while at the same time the collected wisdom of our ancestors which helped the race survive."[42] The "Maat magick" of the Horus/Maat Lodge aims to awaken this future human consciousness through theurgic ritual. As Nema explains,

> Maat Magick developed, in part, from the vision of the probability worlds and communion with our future species-self who calls itself N'Aton. The image I have of N'Aton is an androgynous human, strongly lit from the left, the right side in deep shadow in which various sub-images appear . . . In N'Aton's home [time] line, we've controlled our mutation into a species of double consciousness: the familiar one of individuality and the new telepathic connection among us that constitutes N'Aton.

39. "Zuvuya: An Essay on Aeonics," cited in Karr, *Approaching the Kabbalah of Maat*, 58.

40. *Kairos* is a biblical term for a moment of great change and transition.

41. Karr, *Approaching the Kabbalah of Maat*, 63.

42. Ibid., 64.

If one hungers, all feel it; victims and villains share such intimacy that all pain given is simultaneously felt by the giver. If a mind turns to madness, it's comforted and returned to health by everyone around it . . . Maat Magick aims to accelerate our development into N'Aton since we need that level of intelligence to survive and to reverse the damage we've done to the Earth.[43]

Many of the themes here resemble the Xenofeminist Manifesto—the mutation of identity in the service of a future universality, alienation from our current broken social structure, and a futurist hope in a more fluid, peaceful, and just age to come. The Horus/Maat Lodge's future-oriented esotericism also resembles the late-nineteenth-century French occult theme of the coming Age of the Paraclete, in which the Holy Spirit rules a utopian age in which the fall of humanity is overcome and the universal church of the future replaces corrupt, current-day Christianity.

Most suggestively, this vision of the "homo veritas" of the future also evokes the mid-century Catholic theology of figures such as Teilhard de Chardin, Segundo, and Schillebeeckx. N'Aton is, essentially, a Thelemic version of Teilhard de Chardin's Omega Point, Segundo's "new humanity," and Schillebeeckx's eschatological *humanum*. And the notion of a future Aeon of truth and justice which rushes in from the future bears an uncanny resemblance to Schillebeeckx's declaration that "God is the future of man"—God is "new each moment," a divine reality who comes to us from the sphere of the future. Julia Feder explains that Schillebeeckx's view of the future human being is deeply open-ended, though in some way collective like Nema's N'Aton:

> The statement that God is our future articulates well the relational destiny of humanity without narrowly delineating a positivistic portrait of the humanum. If God is our future, creation has . . . both an open yet also deterministic end.[44]

---

43. Nema, *Maat Magick*, 65–66.
44. Feder, "Directed toward Relationship," 455.

Schillebeeckx has a resolutely pluralist view of the *humanum*, that new human being who dwells in the City of the Silver Star. According to Schillebeeckx, Christian doctrine must "have an orientation towards the future and be open to the sphere of the future"; truth is "something whose fullness belongs to the future; to the extent that its content is already realized, it discloses itself as essentially a promise."[45] As we discussed in the introduction, the *humanum* is a promise of future human fulfillment that, in the present historical context, we can only grasp negatively in our response to negative contrast experiences, experiences of injustice that cause us to irrupt in struggle, fighting to better witness the eschaton that comes to us from the sphere of the future. Through this spirit of struggle, we work to build the City of the Silver Star here on earth.

The Bride's Reception

Our examination of the City of the Silver Star, that Holy City of the future toward which the inner church is questing, and our reflection on its future inhabitants, has now come full circle with our earlier qabalistic explorations.[46] The godform of Maat—which the magicians of the Horus/Maat Lodge see as coming to us from the sphere of the future—can also be identified with the qabalistic Daughter, the final *Hé* of the Tetragrammaton, the element of Earth and the sphere of Malkuth. Nema and the Horus/Maat Lodge derive much of their Aeonic speculations from Frater Achad (Charles Stansfeld Jones), who was the first Thelemite after Aleister Crowley to declare the arrival of the Aeon of Maat.

One must understand the implications of Achad's 1920s qabalistic theories, his 1928 conversion to Roman Catholicism, and his leadership of the Universal Brotherhood, to fully grasp the significance of an early Aeon of truth and justice—the spiritual ideas

---

45. Schillebeeckx, *God the Future of Man*, 36.
46. See chapter 2, "Social Qabalah."

personified by the godform of Maat.⁴⁷ Achad is perhaps uniquely pro-materiality among early-twentieth-century occultists. Unlike various gnostics, Neo-Buddhists, and theosophists of the era, Achad supports a material world that is infused with spirit—one might say sacramentally infused.

Significantly, this fits with Achad's radical qabalistic speculations. Achad's complex vision of the primal fall and eschatological restoration of the Tree of Life resembles a process of cosmic evolution. He has this in common with the modernist Catholic theologians who were current in his day, such as Teilhard de Chardin. In his 1925 book, *The Anatomy of the Body of God*, Achad writes,

> Idealism and Materialism must unite and go hand in hand if a new Civilization is to be built up. The Soul of Humanity is the connecting link. There is nothing to be ashamed of in our material bodies, but they would not be of much use without the Spirit and Will which give them Life and motion. On the other hand we should not be so cowardly and selfish as to desire to be re-absorbed into Spirit, as if the whole Creative Plan were a waste of time, and had better never have been started. No! Let us give thanks in our souls for both body and spirit, using both rightly and to the full extent of our power.⁴⁸

Achad's writings became increasingly oriented toward the immanent fulfillment of the kingdom of God over the course of the 1920s, a view that would be labeled "realized eschatology" in the terms of Christian theology. Again, from *The Anatomy of the Body of God*: "We must enter upon the heritage of Freedom that has been prepared for us in the Father's Kingdom upon Earth"; "In the Name of the True and Living God, let us cease from bloody sacrifice, and start to build a 'Living Temple, not made with hands, eternal in the Heavens'—upon Earth."⁴⁹ The last chapter of the book concludes with the stirring declaration:

---

47. For an overview of Frater Achad's Maatian ideas, see Karr, *Approaching the Kabbalah of Maat*, 28–33.
48. Achad, *Anatomy of the Body of God*, ix–x.
49. Ibid., ix–x.

There is a place prepared for every one of you, Here and Now. There is a place for everything, when all things shall be put in place. Take up your places in the Kingdom of the Ever-Coming Son, fulfill yourselves, in the fulfillment of the Will of God within you, and show those who are still in darkness without, that there is room for all who are prepared to keep their place, and cease from trying to usurp that of others.[50]

Frater Achad's understanding of the incoming kingdom of God results from his interpretation of the cosmic process of Qabalah. The Egyptian godforms in the orthodox Thelemic schema of the Aeons—Isis, Osiris, Horus—correspond to Binah (the Mother), Chokmah (the Father), and Tiphareth (the Son), respectively. Maat completes the sequence of four by representing Malkuth (the Daughter), the material kingdom. The Aeons can also be assigned to the four letters of the Hebrew Tetragrammaton, IHVH—Osiris (I), Isis (H), Horus (V), with Maat (H final) completing the sequence.

As we saw earlier in our reflection on the social Qabalah, in order to restore the Tree of Life to its pre-fall state, the fallen Daughter (H final) must unite with the Son (V) to rise to the level of H prime, installing the Daughter/Malkuth on the throne of Binah, the Mother (H prime). As Achad explains, the Mother then "arouses the active force of THE FATHER, and these twain being UNITED [in Daath, the City of the Silver Star], all is RE-ABSORBED into THE CROWN."[51] Thus the eschatological kingdom is realized on earth, Malkuth being united with Kether in fulfillment of God's plan for creation.

In Catholic theology, this process can be described through the salvation economy of Mary, a daughter of Israel and child of earth, conceiving the Son, the Christos, by the Holy Spirit, then being united with God the Father in her coronation as the queen of heaven in the heavenly Jerusalem. The Son's incarnation thus redeems the material world of Malkuth—represented in microcosm

---

50. Ibid., 110–11.
51. Achad, *Q.B.L. or The Bride's Reception*, 61–62.

by Mary—through the in-breaking of the eschatological kingdom in the event of Jesus Christ. Catholics participate in this reality—the eschaton made present here and now in fulfillment of God's plan—through the theurgy of the Eucharistic Mass.

Numerous orthodox Thelemites have suggested outlandish theories as to why Frater Achad would ever convert to the Roman Catholic Church: insanity, the desire to convert the church to the law of Thelema, or being lost in the Abyss as a Black Brother. Yet Achad himself gives a different explanation of his curious conversion:

> It was necessary for Achad to be led to the opposite Pillar of the Temple there to learn the mysteries of the R[oman] C[atholic] Church. He became an orthodox member of that Church and received his first communion at Midnight Mass, Christmas, 1928. This step, and this alone, led to the opening of the Initiations and Ordeals which were to follow in accordance with *Liber Legis* [Aleister Crowley's Thelemic holy text, better known as *The Book of the Law*].[52]

After coming through these initiatory ordeals, Achad was ready to proclaim the dawning of the Aeon of truth and justice—the eschatological kingdom fulfilled on earth, glyphed in esoteric terms by the goddess Maat, glyphed in the New Testament by John's vision of the New Jerusalem in the Book of Revelation:

> Then I saw a new heaven and a new earth; for the first heaven and the first earth had passed away, and the sea was no more. And I saw the holy city, the new Jerusalem, coming down out of heaven from God, prepared as a bride adorned for her husband.[53]

This is *the bride's reception*—the New Jerusalem come down to earth, the divine united with the material world, the advent of the City of the Silver Star. Indeed, Achad labeled one of the

---

52. Achad, letter to Gerald Yorke and Albert Handel, May 6, 1948, cited in Beta, "Prolegomenon," xxvi–xxvii.

53. Rev 21:1–3 (NRSV).

"Initiations and Ordeals" he experienced, which eventually led to his vision of the Aeon of Maat, "the Arising of the Silver Star."[54]

Significantly, Frater Achad's conversion to Roman Catholicism allowed him to join in the sacramental life of the church. This means he also participated in the Eucharist, with his first Mass being the Mass celebrating the incarnation at Christmas, 1928. The Eucharist is, for Catholics, the kingdom of God made present here on earth, the eschatological reality breaking into our present moment. As the *Catechism of the Catholic Church* states, the Eucharist is "a pledge of future glory," a foretaste of the heavenly banquet to come.[55] Like the in-breaking kingdom of God, rushing in from the future to meet us in our present-day experience of the Eucharist, the Aeon of Maat is a "backwards current," granting us a vision in the here and now of an age in which "we all may become something far greater, something which exists in the form of seeds within us in the eternal Now."[56]

My reading of the Catholic Frater Achad through the lens of the Eucharist—which, as we have seen, situates all other theurgical attempts to further the process of cosmological evolution around the Silver Star of Bethlehem—suggests that the new Aeon of truth and justice *is* here in the present. It is simultaneous with the "force and fire" of the Aeon of Horus—sacramentally, in the Eucharist, through the foretaste we receive here and now of the heavenly banquet that is to come. And as Teilhard de Chardin teaches us, this eschatological transubstantiation includes both the cosmos and human society. The Daughter, the earthly city, is raised to the throne of the Mother, the Father is roused, and the Son of God—the universal commonweal—is born in the midst of the people of earth. As Frater Achad proclaims, drawing on the ancient qabalists, "Kether is in Malkuth and Malkuth is in Kether."[57]

---

54. Beta, "Prolegomenon," xxvii.
55. *Catechism of the Catholic Church*, 1402.
56. Horus-Maat Lodge, "Frequently Asked Questions," para. 10.
57. Achad, *Q.B.L., or The Bride's Reception*, 12.

The Grand Consummation

In the Preparatory Essay of the Bavarian Illuminati, the author states plainly the intellectual framework of that much-maligned society:

> There are certain truths, holy truths, that enlighten man about his past, present, and future condition.—They most certainly exist.—Call them revelation, or what you will.—Whether they are the results of thorough research or communications from the hands of higher beings—enough! Any intelligent man is bound to feel that he requires them, because he remains in doubt about so many things in nature.[58]

In this statement, the historical Illuminati establishes itself as an order concerned with propagating the universal wisdom required for the right ordering of human society, whether that wisdom originates with higher beings, scientific research, or from some other source, sacred or secular.

The idea of a peaceable planetary commonwealth, founded on the universal principles of wisdom enshrined in the world's great religious traditions, and respecting the inalienable rights of all human beings, seems to be a laudable goal. But the Illuminati quickly fell due to infighting, political repression, and the usual institutional failures—and it is now a byword for any would-be conspiratorial society that secretly plots a New World Order, from the instigators of the French Revolution to reptilian shapeshifters from outer space. The historical Illuminati's vision of a universal utopian society founded on reason has become a superstitious mélange of dystopian nightmares, usually involving some combination of the Vatican and the British Royal Family.

Perhaps it was destined to be so. Practically any group whose goals include the universal reformation of society is pegged at one point or another as sectarian, intolerant, or potentially evil, either politically or supernaturally. The Gothic novels of eighteenth- and nineteenth-century England had their cruel

---

58. Markner and Wäges, *Secret School of Wisdom*, 47.

Jesuit Illuminati Freemasons as the villains, inciting rebellion between bouts of sexual depravity and decadence (never mind the fact that the Illuminati and the Jesuits were essentially archnemeses). The pulp fiction of the United States combined (and still combines) some assortment of Catholics, racial minorities, and communists as the enemies of our moral and political order. If the Black Lives Matter movement hasn't yet been linked in any conspiracy theories to the lizard people, dangerous communists, or the Illuminati, it is only a matter of time.

Like the hybrid human-alien antagonists of H. P. Lovecraft's weird fiction, working against the white Anglo-Saxon protagonists and their sedate New England reason to summon the Deep Ones back from their slumber to retake the Earth as their rightful home, the political, moral, and cultural imaginary of most societies usually includes a mythical version of the Other and its nightside encroachment upon the civilized world's daylight consciousness.

It is a radical act, then, for occultists like Kenneth Grant, Nema, and the Horus/Maat Lodge to valorize the ontologically Other, to suggest that the Great Work includes the mutation of human consciousness into something beyond, something that undermines the certainties and pieties of not only our present-day civilization, but also the very notion of the human itself.

Yet political utility is only one reason for this principle of reappropriating otherness. To return to the quote from the Illuminati, that order saw itself not as proposing radical, artificial doctrines as a replacement for the common sense of traditional society, but as reforming society along the lines of "certain truths, holy truths"[59] that exist as the primordial bedrock of human life, as embedded in the "soil of sentiency,"[60] to use a phrase from Grant's *Outside the Circles of Time*, or in the One Idea of God for God's creation, to use the concepts of the social Qabalah.

Or, as Edward Schillebeeckx puts it, humanity's existential questions are "sustained by the reality of creation" and thus, implicitly, "rooted in the soil of all religious experience: God's

---

59. Markner and Wäges, *Secret School of Wisdom*, 47.
60. Grant, *Outside the Circles of Time*, 12.

sovereign and unexpected act of creation which is not overcome by our sinfulness."[61] This "superior power of God's good act of creation arouses in us the quest for the real basis of the datum of experience that people, despite everything . . . continue their trust that goodness and not evil must have the last word."[62] As a Catholic, for Schillebeeckx the Christian gospel "extends this 'must have' to 'will have,'" but even so, without humanity's prior "must have," "the Christian 'will have' would be unintelligible."[63]

There is, then—according to Catholic theology and occultism alike—a pagan wisdom, a natural religion, embedded in the soil of humanity's religious experience. The experience of this reality is primary to all doctrinal speculation, philosophical reasoning and, according to Schillebeeckx, to all activist attempts at improving the condition of humanity on this planet. For Kenneth Grant and other occultists, it comes from beyond human consciousness, and will result in the cosmic Aeonic evolution of our race, the "homo veritas" who dwells in the City of the Silver Star. The Illuminati didn't care whether it came from higher beings or from natural reason; all that mattered was the fact that our civilization should be refounded upon it.

The conflation of the Illuminati, the left-hand path of occultism, the Jesuits, and our alien overlords from Sirius, starts to seem less odd when considered from this angle. All the most radical theologies and philosophies point to the same essential idea: humanity and human civilization must evolve beyond its present impasse, and this evolution will be rooted in the telluric soil of our primordial being. For the political Powers That Be, this idea is dangerous and Other, and is usefully mythicized as an alien invasion, a Freemasonic plot, or a Vatican conspiracy.

The drive to form a planetary commonwealth, to complete the Great Work, to reach the grand consummation that will render us alien to our current fallen human forms—what Frater Achad called "the Universal Terrestrial Realization of the Ideal [the One Idea],

---

61. Schillebeeckx, *Understanding of Faith*, 98.
62. Ibid., 98.
63. Ibid., 98.

the deliberate carrying into effect and bringing to full fruition of the Divine and macrocosmic Purposes,"[64] what Kenneth Grant called "the Arachnean Aeon of the Outer Ones" which will span "the gulfs of Time and Space" and in which "the 'Great Race' will be exalted," and what I call the City of the Silver Star—remains a dangerous and necessary idea, an idea which has the potential to transfigure the very nature of humanity and human civilization.[65]

As Schillebeeckx knew, we can only catch glimpses of this future *humanum* in our active responses to injustice, like viewing the negative of a photograph. As Grant knew, we can only see it in shadow. We can only imagine, through our wildest esoteric speculations, what being a citizen of the City of Silver Star will mean, what being transubstantiated into the cosmic Christ will look like. But as the First Epistle of John proclaims, "Beloved, we are God's children now; what we will be has not yet been revealed. What we do know is this: when Christ is revealed, we will be like him, for we will see him as he is."[66]

---

64. Grant, *Beyond the Mauve Zone*, 149.
65. Starr, *Unknown God*, 149.
66. 1 John 3:2, adapted from the NRSV.

Conclusion

WESTERN ESOTERICISM HAS BEEN a major part of the U. S. religious landscape since before the founding of our nation. It has also frequently been denigrated by more traditional religious authorities, or relegated to the paranoid realm of conspiracy theory or 1980s-era satanic panic. Mitch Horowitz—author of *Occult America*—writes in *Salon* that the influence of esotericism on Americans has more to do with the American character than any secret Illuminati plot to build a nefarious new world order:

> Rather than fomenting secrecy or subterfuge, America's embrace of esotericism is often characterized by a chin-out earnestness, something that many observers and conspiracy-mongers miss . . . Today, cable television producers and radio hosts often urge me to postulate some kind of occult "pact" between the Bushes and the dark side (cue up Skull and Bones). But such things are fantasy. The truth is, Americans have always been, well, a little strange. As a historian, I feel affection for that aspect of American life. Shadowy figures have long hung around the fringes of power in many nations; but rarely have they done so with the ingenuousness and transparency of those I've been considering.[1]

Rather than suggesting that American esotericism is inherently liberal or conservative, inherently tied to liberative or reactionary politics, Horowitz proposes that our "belief in the protection of the individual search for meaning," even expressed in terms of "esoteric and unusual religious ideas in our political culture," is a fact that

---

1. Horowitz, "Steve Bannon and the Occult," paras. 13, 21.

"unites us across our fractured political divide."[2] Esotericists can be right-wing populists like Steve Bannon (who frequently cites the ideas of Italian esotericist and Nazi sympathizer Julius Evola), but they can also be flower-children living in anarchist communes, twenty-somethings with Tarot card tattoos, and military service people who choose occult symbols for their gravestones in Arlington National Cemetery. Americans are nothing if not eclectic in our religious beliefs and in our politics.

Recently, the phenomenon of Donald Trump-binding witches in Brooklyn's hipster neighborhoods like Bushwick and Williamsburg have made mainstream news as evidence of an occult revival among left-leaning millennials who are searching for spiritual resources to cope with or react to our catastrophic political landscape.[3] These young people belong to the demographic that has increasingly rejected organized religion, but has also found that pure scientism or atheism haven't fulfilled their spiritual needs. They thus seek solace in the more outlandish, renegade, or gender-nonconforming realms of occultism and neopaganism.

My own experience suggests that this is an accurate diagnosis of a subset of modern esotericists, but what the *New York Times* op-ed writers and spiritual gurus both fail to do is to find some way to harness this energy for building a broad social movement to actually struggle for the restructuring of a morally bankrupt society. After all, many of the boho queer genderfluid artist pagans I know who are into hexing Donald Trump are also members of the ranks of the poor and dispossessed—they just haven't been organized effectively in any way that actually relates to their experience of the world and their nascent esoteric spiritualities.

If the meaning of esotericism in American politics is multivalent, how can esoteric spiritualities, however faddish they might be in the current religious landscape, contribute to the goal of building a universality from below, a City of the Silver Star, a new humanity in the service of the movement to end poverty, racism, militarism, ecological devastation, and other attendant evils? The

2. Ibid., para. 21.
3. See, for example, Gault, "Use This Spell to Bind Trump and His Cronies."

common image of esoteric movements—whether it is secret organizations like the Illuminati, fraternal societies like Freemasonry, or magical orders like the Hermetic Order of the Golden Dawn—is of mysterious masked figures practicing solemn rituals, or powerful old men meeting in smoke-filled rooms, planning the future of the new world order. However, as Horowitz's article suggests, the truth of these movements is both more pedestrian and potentially more radical. Esotericism has kept alive certain threads of religious and spiritual attainment that have been excluded from the mainstream religions of the Western world. The fraternities, orders, and societies that continue to pass on this rejected knowledge have frequently served as laboratories of new forms of social organization, spiritualities, and political formations.

Until the recent development of esoteric studies, however, esotericism and esoteric groups were largely ignored in the academy. Even now, many esotericists tend to focus on the more mystical or intellectual aspects of esotericism, rather than its social impact. More mainstream religious studies scholars and theologians, meanwhile, continue to consider esoteric movements as outside the scope of their studies. Esotericism is not, after all, religion—it is on the periphery of religion, existing in the spheres of the irrational, the rejected, or the occult.

Yet the introduction to the Kairos Center's *The Spirit of Struggle* deconstructs the common notion of "religion," explaining that "even the term 'religions' can be a highly contested and problematic one."[4] Rather than focusing on the abstract high theology of world religions, the contributors to *The Spirit of Struggle* concentrate their scholarship on "the 'lived religion' of people fighting for social justice."[5] The essay continues:

> Putting aside preconceived ideas of what is and isn't "religion" makes possible going beyond only or mainly organized creeds and institutional forms of religion to explore and learn from all beliefs and practices that

---

4. Kairos Center, *Spirit of Struggle*, 1.
5. Ibid., 1.

point to a transcendent or deeper source of meaning and power.[6]

In terms of esotericism, by bracketing debates about what is and isn't religion, we can expand the scope of our education to include those forms of rejected beliefs and practices which might point to a "transcendent or deeper source of meaning and power," but which do not fit the mold of traditional religion. We can begin to pose the questions asked in *The Spirit of Struggle* to Western esotericism and its relation to and potential for popular social movements:

> How do these movements, and their participants, define the source(s) of meaning, power, and inspiration in their work? Are there collective definitions of these values and where do these come from? . . . What kind of teachings, symbols, rituals and practices are used to help sustain and inspire those involved in diverse struggles for social justice?[7]

In the above chapters, we explored numerous examples of Western esoteric movements—and their teachings, symbols, rituals and practices—in dialogue with Christian liberation theology in order to better understand how these movements might provide meaning, power, and inspiration for broad, liberation theology-influenced social movements like the new Poor People's Campaign. As the above quote suggests, we asked whether the Western esoteric tradition, interpreted through a liberationist framework, might help to "sustain and inspire those involved in diverse struggles for social justice," in what the Rosicrucians might call the quest for universal reformation.

In order to go to the fringes of esoteric and occult spirituality and emerge with new data for theological reflection, especially in order to put such data in conversation with liberative theologies and social movements that are themselves radical, I might sometimes have appeared, in the above, to have gone off the rails

6. Ibid., 2.
7. Ibid., 2.

in terms of one coherent line of thought or ideology—if there were any rails to begin with in the realm of the esoteric, the occult, and the utopian.

But one conclusion emerges as the central organizing principle of the reflections offered here, cutting across many traditions and currents in order to express the One Idea of the God who is our liberator: that the inner, spiritual church that Rev. Dr. Martin Luther King Jr. speaks of as the heart of movements of the poor and dispossessed to break the chains of their oppression, is also the inner church that the esotericists, occultists, and mystics speak of, the hidden assembly consisting of all who have conformed themselves to God's vision of freedom and liberation, and who struggle to enact that vision in the world and in human societies. The inner church is truly the hope of the world.

Furthermore, the guiding lights of this inner church are those personal and transpersonal beings who have made themselves perfect channels of God's liberating light, allowing the One Idea to unfold in the created cosmos. The paragon of these "unknown cadre," for Christian theologians, activists, and esotericists alike, is Jesus Christ, the incarnation of the One Idea or the Logos in our human history, the Silver Star of Bethlehem around which the whole cosmos reorients itself in its grand consummation.

Yet many legitimate expressions of the One Idea can be found in the world's historical struggles for liberation—and these include religious expressions which are usually considered fringe, esoteric, or occult. All of these expressions across human history constitute glimpses of the glorified *humanum*, the citizens of the City of the Silver Star who have been freed from the chains of social oppression through the blossoming of a new society and a new humanity. These shadows of a future aeon can be seen darkly in the magic mirror of Western esotericism. If there is a successful unity to my reflections here, it is to be found in this deep conviction.

Bibliography

Achad, Frater. *The Anatomy of the Body of God*. New York: Samuel Weiser, 1973.
———. *The Egyptian Revival, or, The Ever-Coming Son in the Light of the Tarot*. New York: Samuel Weiser, 1973.
———. *Q. B. L., or The Bride's Reception*. New York: Samuel Weiser, 1972.
———. "The Silver Postmesospheric—The Pivotal Man." Typescript in author's collection.
Avanessian, Armen, et al. "#Accelerationism: Remembering the Future." http://criticallegalthinking.com/2014/02/10/accelerationism-remembering-future/.
Bahrim, Dragos. "The Anthropic Cosmology of St. Maximus the Confessor." *Journal for Interdisciplinary Research on Religion and Science* 3 (2008) 11–37.
Barber II, William J., and Jonathan Wilson-Hartgrove. *The Third Reconstruction: Moral Mondays, Fusion Politics, and the Rise of a New Justice Movement*. Boston: Beacon, 2016.
Barnes, Adam, and Shailly Gupta Barnes. "'America, You Must be Born Again!': Rev. Dr. Martin Luther King Jr., Religion, and Social Change." https://kairoscenter.org/mlk-religion-social-change/.
Bates, David. "The Mystery of Truth: Louis Claude de Saint-Martin's Enlightened Mysticism." *Journal of the History of Ideas*, 61.4 (2000) 635–55.
Beta, Hymenaeus. "Prolegomenon." In *Liber Aleph*, 2nd ed., by Aleister Crowley, xiii–xxxii. York Beach, ME: 1992.
Case, Paul Foster. *The True and Invisible Rosicrucian Order*. York Beach, ME: Weiser, 1989.
Catechism of the Catholic Church. New York: Doubleday, 1995.
Chaitow, Sasha. "Making the Invisible Visible: Péladan's Artistic Revolution Meets the 21st Century." In *The Fenris Wolf 7*, edited by Carl Abrahamsson, 17–37. Stockholm: Edda, 2014.
Cherubim, David. "The Golden Dawn and the Secret Chiefs." http://daktologistindustries.com/totse_archive/en/religion/the_occult/163662.html.
Cicero, Chic, and Sandra Tabatha Cicero. *The Essential Golden Dawn: An Introduction to High Magic*. Woodbury, MN: Llewellyn, 2015.

BIBLIOGRAPHY

———. *Self-Initiation into the Golden Dawn Tradition: A Complete Curriculum of Study for Both the Solitary Magician and the Working Magical Group*. St. Paul, MN: Llewellyn, 1995.

Comenius, Jan Amos. *Panergesia or Universal Awakening*. Translated by A. M. O. Dobbie. Warwickshire, UK: Peter I. Drinkwater, 1990.

Cone, James. *A Black Theology of Liberation*. Maryknoll, NY: Orbis, 1990.

———. *God of the Oppressed*. Maryknoll, NY: Orbis, 1997.

Cox, Larry. "The Power of Religion and Human Rights: Keynote Speech at the 2017 Bernstein Symposium at Yale University." https://kairoscenter.org/wp-content/uploads/2017/07/The-Power-of-Religion-and-Human-Rights.pdf.

Crowley, Aleister. "Liber Israfel *sub figura LXIV*." https://hermetic.com/crowley/libers/lib64.

———. *Magick: Liber ABA*. York Beach, ME: Weiser, 1997.

———. "On the Powers of Number." *Force & Fire* 1 (2002) 3–6.

Cselényi, István. *The Maternal Face of God? Explorations in Catholic Sophiology*. Kettering, OH: Angelico, 2017.

Dear, John. "The World—and Word—According to William Stringfellow." *On the Road to Peace* (blog), *National Catholic Reporter*, November 12, 2013. https://www.ncronline.org/blogs/road-peace/world-and-word-according-william-stringfellow.

Dellinger, Drew. "The Ecological King: A Vision for Our Times." *IONS* (blog), January 16, 2017. http://noetic.org/blog/communications-team/ecological-king-vision.

Duncalf, Frederic. "The Peasants' Crusade." *The American Historical Review* 26.3 (1921) 440–53.

Eckhart, Meister. *Selected Writings*. Translated by Oliver Davies. New York: Penguin, 1994.

Faivre, Antoine. *Access to Western Esotericism*. Albany, NY: State University of New York Press, 1994.

———. *Theosophy, Imagination, Tradition: Studies in Western Esotericism*. Albany, NY: State University of New York Press, 2000.

"Fama Fraternitatis." In *The Rosicrucian Manuscripts*, edited by Benedict J. Williamson, 98–117. Arlington, VA: Invisible College, 2002.

Feder, Julia. "Directed toward Relationship: William Stoeger's Immanent Directionality and Edward Schillebeeckx's Mystical Eschatology." *Theological Studies* 78.2 (2017) 447–61.

Ficino, Marsilio. *Three Books on Life: A Critical Edition and Translation with Introduction and Notes*. Edited and translated by Carol V. Kaske and John R. Clark. Tempe, AZ: Renaissance Society of America, 1998.

Fortune, Dion. *The Mystical Qabalah*. San Francisco: Weiser, 1998.

Galloway, Alexander R. "Brometheanism." http://cultureandcommunication.org/galloway/brometheanism.

Gault, Matthew. "Use this Spell to Bind Trump and His Cronies." https://medium.com/defiant/use-this-spell-to-bind-trump-and-his-cronies-a5b6298f5c69.

Gilbert, R. A. "The Lost Stepchild: The Tale of the Societas Rosicruciana in America." http://www.sria.org/the-lost-stepchild-the-tale-of-the-societas-rosicruciana-in-america.

Goodrick-Clarke, Nicholas. *The Western Esoteric Traditions: A Historical Introduction.* Oxford: Oxford University Press, 2008.

Grant, Kenneth. *Beyond the Mauve Zone.* London: Starfire, 2015.

———. *The Magical Revival.* London: Starfire, 2010.

———. *Outside the Circles of Time.* London: Starfire, 2008.

Gutiérrez, Gustavo. *A Theology of Liberation: History, Politics, and Salvation.* Maryknoll, NY: Orbis, 1971.

Gutiérrez, Gustavo, and Paul Farmer. *In the Company of the Poor: Conversations with Dr. Paul Farmer and Fr. Gustavo Gutiérrez.* Maryknoll, NY: Orbis, 2013. Kindle.

Hackett, David G. *That Religion in Which All Men Agree: Freemasonry in American Culture.* Berkeley: University of California Press, 2014.

Hall, Manly P. *Orders of Universal Reformation: Utopias.* Los Angeles: Philosophical Research Society, 1976.

Harding, Vincent. *Martin Luther King: The Inconvenient Hero.* Maryknoll, NY: Orbis, 2008.

Heiser, James D. *Prisci Theologi and the Hermetic Reformation in the Fifteenth Century.* Malone, TX: Repristination, 2011.

Heltzel, Peter Goodwin. "The Inner Church is the Hope for the World: The Pietist Impulse in the Theology of Martin Luther King Jr." In *Pietist Impulse in Christianity*, edited by Christian T. Collins Winn et al., 269–81. Cambridge: James Clarke & Co, 2012.

Horowitz, Mitch. "Steve Bannon and the Occult: The Right Wing's Long, Strange Love Affair with New Age Mysticism." *Salon* (April 17, 2017). https://www.salon.com/2017/04/23/steve-bannon-and-the-occult-the-right-wings-long-strange-love-affair-with-new-age-mysticism/.

Horus-Maat Lodge. "Frequently Asked Questions." http://horusmaatlodge.com/about/faq.html.

Kaczynski, Richard. *Perdurabo: The Life of Aleister Crowley.* Tempe, AZ: New Falcon, 2002.

Kairos Center. "Breaking News! Rev. Dr. William Barber Stepping Up to Join the Leadership of the New Poor People's Campaign." https://kairoscenter.org/breaking-news-rev-dr-william-barber-transition.

———."Dr. King's Speech." https://kairoscenter.org/new-ppc-bible-study-2-life-abundant/.

———. "The Rejected Will Lead the Revival: Congratulations to Bishop William J. Barber, II!" https://kairoscenter.org/congratulations-bishop-william-barber/.

———. *The Spirit of Struggle: Writings on Religions and Human Rights.* http://www.kairoscenter.org/wp-content/uploads/2015/11/Sprit-of-Struggle-online.pdf.

———. "When Jesus Says Love He Means It: Excerpts from Martin Luther King Jr.'s 1967 Frogmore Speech on its 50th Anniversary." https://kairoscenter.org/mlk-frogmore-staff-retreat-speech-anniversary/.

Karr, Don. *Approaching the Kabbalah of Maat.* York Beach, ME: Black Jackal, 2013.

The King Center. "Freemasons, Prince Hall Grand Lodge." http://www.thekingcenter.org/archive/theme/428.

King Jr., Martin Luther. "Letter from a Birmingham Jail." https://www.africa.upenn.edu/Articles_Gen/Letter_Birmingham.html.

———. *The Trumpet of Conscience.* Boston: Beacon, 2010.

———. *Where Do We Go from Here? Chaos or Community.* New York: Bantam, 1968.

———. "Where Do We Go from Here?" In *A Testament of Hope: The Essential Writings and Speeches of Martin Luther King Jr.*, edited by James M. Washington, 245–52. New York: HarperOne, 1986.

Laboria Cuboniks. *Xenofeminism: A Politics for Alienation.* http://www.laboriacuboniks.net/.

Leadbeater, Charles Webster. *The Science of the Sacraments.* Dominica: European-American University Press, 2007. Electronic edition.

Lévi, Eliphas. *The Book of Splendors: The Inner Mysteries of Qabalism.* York Beach, ME: Samuel Weiser, 1984.

———. *The Doctrine and Ritual of High Magic: A New Translation.* Translated by John Michael Greer and Mark Anthony Mikituk. New York: TarcherPerigee, 2017.

Lorente-Bull, Darren, and Julian Rees. *More Light: Today's Freemasonry for Men and Women.* Surrey, UK: Hexalpha, 2017.

Markner, Reinhard, and Josef Wäges, eds. *The Secret School of Wisdom: The Authentic Rituals and Doctrines of the Illuminati.* Translated by Jeva Singh-Anand. Malta: Lewis Masonic, 2015.

Maximillian of Kolbe. *The Kolbe Reader: The Writings of St. Maximillian of Kolbe.* Edited by Anselm W. Romb. Libertyville, IL: Marytown, 2007.

McGovern, Una. *Chambers Dictionary of the Unexplained.* Edinburgh: Chambers, 2007.

McIntosh, Alastair. "Engaging Walter Wink's Powers—An Activist's Testimony." In *Enigmas and Powers: Engaging the Work of Walter Wink for Classroom, Church, and World*, edited by D. Seiple and Frederick W. Weidmann, 101–12. Eugene, OR: Pickwick, 2008.

McIntosh, Christopher. *Eliphas Lévi and the French Occult Revival.* Albany, NY: State University of New York Press, 2011.

———. *The Rosy Cross Unveiled: The History, Mythology and Rituals of an Occult Order.* Wellingborough, UK: Aquarian, 1980.

Milbank, John. "Foreword." In *Introducing Radical Orthodoxy: Mapping a Post-Secular Theology*, by James K. A. Smith, 11–20. Grand Rapids, MI: Baker Academic, 2004.

Nema. *Maat Magick: A Guide to Self-Initiation*. York Beach, ME: Samuel Weiser, 1995.

Omicron, Otto. "Commentary on Liber Israfel sub Figura LXIV." https://everything2.com/title/Commentary+on+Liber+Israfel+sub+Figura+LXIV.

Papus. *Elementary Treatise on Practical Magic*. Translated by Piers A. Vaughn. Bayonne, NJ: Rose Circle, 2017.

Perisho, Steve. "Semper reformanda." http://spu.libguides.com/DCL2017/Reformation#s-lg-box-wrapper-18675181.

Pike, Albert. *Morals and Dogma of a Council of Kadosh*. Unspeakable, 2008. http://melchizedek-sks.synthasite.com/resources/3457792-Morals-and-Dogma-of-a-Council-of-Kadosh.pdf.

Poor People's Campaign. *The Souls of Poor Folk: Auditing America 50 Years After the Poor People's Campaign Challenged Racism, Poverty, the War Economy/Militarism and Our National Morality*. https://poorpeoplescampaign.org/index.php/audit/.

"Pope Francis: The Church's Mercy is for Everyone." *Catholic News Agency* (Nov. 12, 2016). https://www.catholicnewsagency.com/news/pope-francis-the-churchs-mercy-is-for-everyone-46009.

Recnartus, Frater. "Pansophy." *Pansophic Intellectualizer* 3 (1937) 142–57.

Regardie, Israel. *A Garden of Pomegranates: An Outline of the Qabalah*. St. Paul, MN: Llewellyn, 1985.

———. *The Golden Dawn*. St. Paul, MN: Llewellyn, 1989.

———. *The Middle Pillar: The Balance Between Mind and Magic*. Edited by Chic Cicero and Sandra Tabatha Cicero. Woodbury, MN: Llewellyn, 1998.

Reilly, Gerald. "Freemasonry: 'A Peculiar System of Morality?'" *Pietre-Stones Review of Freemasonry* (Winter 2007). http://www.freemasons-freemasonry.com/column1207.html.

Russell, Norman. *The Doctrine of Deification in the Greek Patristic Tradition*. Oxford: Oxford University Press, 2006.

de Saint-Martin, Louis Claude. *Theosophic Correspondence*. Translated and edited by Edward Burton Penny. Pasadena, CA: Theosophical University Press, 1949.

Schillebeeckx, Edward. *Christ the Sacrament of the Encounter with God*. New York: Sheed and Ward, 1963.

———. "Erfahrung und Glaube." In *Christlicher Glaube in Moderner Gesellschaft*. Enzyklopädische Bibliothek in 30 Teilbänden, vol. 25, edited by F. Böcke et al., 73–116. Freiburg, Germany: Herder, 1980.

———. *God among Us: The Gospel Proclaimed*. New York: Crossroad, 1998.

———. *God the Future of Man*. Translated by N. D. Smith. New York: Sheed and Ward, 1968.

———. *Interim Report on the Books Jesus & Christ*. New York: Crossroad, 1981.

———. *The Understanding of Faith: Interpretation and Criticism*. Translated by N. D. Smith. New York: Seabury, 1974.

Segundo, Juan Luis. *Theology for Artisans of a New Humanity, Vol. 1: The Community Called Church*. Maryknoll, NY: Orbis, 1973.

———. *Theology for Artisans of a New Humanity, Vol. 2: Grace and the Human Condition*. Maryknoll, NY: Orbis, 1973.

Shaw, Gregory. *Theurgy and the Soul: The Neoplatonism of Iamblichus*. University Park, PA: Pennsylvania State University Press, 1995.

Simut, Corneliu C. *The Ontology of the Church in Hans Küng*. Oxford: Peter Lang, 2007.

Snell, Merwin-Marie. "Transcendental Monism." *Mind Magazine* 13.2 (Feb 1904) 149–56. Typescript copy in author's collection.

Sölle, Dorothee. *The Silent Cry: Mysticism and Resistance*. Minneapolis: Fortress, 2001.

Srnicek, Nick, and Alex Williams. "#Accelerate Manifesto for an Accelerationist Politics." http://criticallegalthinking.com/2013/05/14/accelerate-manifesto-for-an-accelerationist-politics/.

Starr, Martin P. *The Unknown God: W.T. Smith and the Thelemites*. Bolingbrook, IL: Teitan, 2003.

Stringfellow, William. *Free in Obedience*. Eugene, OR: Wipf & Stock, 2006.

———. *William Stringfellow: Essential Writings*. Edited by Bill Wylie-Kellermann. Maryknoll, NY: Orbis, 2013.

Strube, Julian. "Socialist Religion and the Emergence of Occultism: A Genealogical Approach to Socialism and Secularization in 19th-century France." *Religion* 46:3 (2016) 359–88.

Stuart, Elizabeth. "Making No Sense: Liturgy as Queer Space." In *Dancing Theology in Fetish Boots: Essays in Honour of Marcella Althaus-Reid*, edited by Lisa Isherwood and Mark D. Jordan, 113–23. London: SCM, 2010.

Teilhard de Chardin, Pierre. *The Divine Milieu*. New York: Harper Perennial, 2001.

———. *The Making of a Mind: Letters from a Solider-Priest, 1914–1919*. New York: Harper and Row, 1965.

Thunberg, Lars. *Microcosm and Mediator: The Theological Anthropology of Maximus the Confessor*. Chicago: Open Court, 1995.

Versluis, Arthur. *Wisdom's Children: A Christian Esoteric Tradition*. Albany, NY: State University of New York Press, 1999.

Von Eckartshausen, Karl. *The Cloud upon the Sanctuary*. Translated by Isabel de Stieger. Middletown, DE: Azafran, 2016.

Waite, A. E. *Grade of Practicus*. Privately printed. 1916.

———. *The Secret Tradition in Freemasonry*. Vol. 1. London: Rebman Limited, 1911.

———. "The Templar Orders in Freemasonry: An Historical Consideration of their Origin and Development." In *A.E. Waite: Words from a Masonic Mystic*, edited by Michael R. Poll, locations 1812–2113 of 2116. New Orleans: Cornerstone, 2006. Kindle.

———. *The Third Order of the Rosy Cross: World of Creation, Part I. The Ceremony of Reception in the Portal of the Third Order, Being the Second Portal Grade.* Privately printed. 1916.

Walker, Corey D. B. *A Noble Fight: African American Freemasonry and the Struggle for Democracy in America.* Chicago: University of Illinois Press, 2010.

Wessel-McCoy, Colleen. "Fifty Years Since 'Beyond Vietnam.'" https://kairoscenter.org/fifty-years-since-beyond-vietnam.

———. "'Freedom Church of the Poor': Martin Luther King Jr.'s Vision for a Poor People's Campaign and its Lessons for Today." PhD diss., Union Theological Seminary, 2017.

———. "When Jesus Says Love He Means it: Excerpts from Martin Luther King Jr.'s 1967 Frogmore speech on its 50th Anniversary." https://kairoscenter.org/mlk-frogmore-staff-retreat-speech-anniversary/.

Wildoak, Peregrin. *By Names and Images: Bringing the Golden Dawn to Life.* Cheltenham, UK: Skylight, 2012.

"Word Symbolism." *The Shrine of Wisdom* 5.18 (1923) 43–8.

Yates, Frances A. *Giordano Bruno and the Hermetic Tradition.* London: Routledge, 1964.

———. *The Rosicrucian Enlightenment.* London: Routledge, 1972.

Yeats, William Butler. "Rosa Alchemica." Corpus of Electronic Texts Edition. https://celt.ucc.ie/published/E890001-001.html.

Index

A∴A∴, 36n26, 69, 72, 75, 87n10
Abernathy, Ralph, 99–100
accelerationism, 105–109
Achad, Frater, 10n21, 18n3, 20, 39,
    50-51, 122–26, 129–30, 137
akasha, 47
alchemy, 30, 60, 77, 85, 98
Andreae, Johann Valentin, 3–4
Arnold, Gottfried, 85
Avanessian, Armen, 105, 137

Bacon, Francis, 3
Barber II, William J., 94, 113,
    115n33, 116, 137
Barth, Karl, 1, 43
Binah. *See* Qabalah.
Boehme, Jacob, 84–85
Bonus Army, 95–96
Bruno, Giordano, 2–4

Cabala. *See* Qabalah.
Campanella, Tommaso, 3–4
capitalism, 45, 48, 51, 105, 107–108
Case, Paul Foster, 71–72, 137
Catholicism, 1–2, 5, 22, 34n20,
    37, 55–56, 62, 66, 73, 77,
    121–26, 128–29, 137
    *Catechism of the Catholic
    Church*, 55–56, 126, 137
Chaitow, Sasha, 10, 137
Cherubim, David, 71, 137
Chesed. *See* Qabalah.
chivalry, 97–99, 102

Chokmah. *See* Qabalah.
Christ, Jesus, 2, 18, 28–31, 33,
    40–44, 55–69, 71–72, 74,
    76–79, 87, 89, 91, 102–103,
    118, 124–25, 130, 135
Christmas, 55, 58, 68, 125–26
Christology, 33, 35, 43
Cicero, Chic, 32, 137–38
Cicero, Sandra Tabatha, 32, 137–38
collective unconscious, 48, 120
Comenius, John Amos, 3–4, 9–10,
    85, 138
Cone, James, 6, 42–44, 138
Cox, Larry, 112, 138
Crowley, Aleister, 5, 18n3, 35–36,
    39, 67, 69, 72-78, 86, 87n10,
    118–19, 122, 125, 138
Crusades, 95–96
crucifixion, 55, 61, 68, 77, 89

Daath. *See* Qabalah.
de Saint-Martin, Louis Claude, 85,
    91, 137, 141
Declaration of Independence, 114
Defenestrate-Bascule, Orryelle, 119
Dellinger, Drew, 68n4, 138

Enlightenment, 5, 110–11, 114–16
eschatology, 7, 12, 28, 32, 36, 39n37,
    40, 42, 51, 56, 58, 62, 73,
    99–101, 120–26
Eucharist, 55–57, 59–61, 66, 73,
    125–26

INDEX

Faivre, Antoine, 4n12, 8–9, 138
Fellowship of the Rosy Cross, 60–61, 70–71, 142–43
Ficino, Marsilio, 2, 4, 138
Fortune, Dion, 21, 40–41, 44, 46, 138
Francis (Pope), 38, 141
Freemasonry, 5, 38n31, 58, 97–98, 114–18, 133, 139–43

Galloway, Alexander R., 109–110, 138
Garden of Eden, 49
Geburah. *See* Qabalah.
Gilbert, R.A., 86, 139
Goodrick-Clarke, Nicholas, 84–85, 139
Golden Dawn. *See* Hermetic Order of the Golden Dawn.
Grant, Kenneth, 11–13, 39, 128–30, 139
Gutiérrez, Gustavo, 6, 8, 89–90, 139

Hall, Manly P., 1n4, 3–4, 139
Heltzel, Peter, 83–84, 86, 139
Hermetic Order of the Golden Dawn, 20, 30, 32, 36, 40, 42, 50, 65–66, 69–71, 75, 78, 86, 87n10, 103–104, 109, 118–19, 133, 137–38, 141, 143
Hermetic Reformation, 1, 139
Hermeticism, 2, 85
Hod. *See* Qabalah.
Holy City. *See* New Jerusalem.
Holy Spirit, 4, 34–36, 63, 77–78, 94–95, 121, 124
Horowitz, Mitch, 131, 133, 139
Horus-Maat Lodge, 119–22, 128, 134, 139
human rights, 6, 91, 93n32, 104, 111–12, 114, 116–17, 119
humanum, 7, 12, 41, 103, 104, 121–22, 130, 135

Illuminati, 5, 127–29, 131, 133, 140
Immaculate Conception, 34–35, 64, 66
Ingalls, Margaret. *See* Nema.
inner church, 37, 69, 83–91, 93, 99, 101–102, 104, 122, 135

Jesuits, 128-29
John, Gospel of, 17, 19, 21–22, 26, 33
Jones, Charles Stansfeld. *See* Achad, Frater.

Kairos Center, 6n13, 104n8, 105, 109, 112, 133, 139
Karr, Don, 119–20, 123n47, 140
Kether. *See* Qabalah.
King Jr., Martin Luther, 6, 28, 31, 37, 40, 68–69, 83–84, 86, 88–102, 104–106, 135, 137–40, 143
Knights Templar, 96–97
Küng, Hans, 1, 142

Laboria Cuboniks, 110, 113, 140
Leadbeater, C.W., 55, 57, 140
Lévi, Eliphas, 22–25, 37–38, 40, 58–59, 140
liberation theology, 5–8, 11, 42, 61n22, 89, 134
Logos, 17–23, 26, 33, 71–72, 76–78, 102, 135
Lopukhin, Ivan Vladimirovich, 85
Lovecraft, H.P., 128

Maat, 39, 119–26, 128
macrocosm and microcosm, 2, 5, 10, 17, 19–20, 25, 31–32, 36, 44, 46–48, 64–66, 124, 130
Malkuth. *See* Qabalah.
Maximillian of Kolbe, 34–35, 140
Maximus the Confessor, 21, 31–32, 65, 137, 142

McIntosh, Christopher, 22n15, 86, 140
Milbank, John, 56, 59–60, 141
mystical theology, 6, 31

N'Aton, 120–121
National Union of the Homeless, 104
Nema, 119–22, 128, 141
Neoplatonism, 1–2, 32, 142
Netzach. *See* Qabalah.
New Jerusalem, 51, 98–103, 125
New World Order, 127, 131, 133
New York City, 6, 47, 92

Omega Point, 61–62, 64–65, 67–69, 121
Omicron, Otto, 74–75, 141
Ordo Templi Orientis, 5

pansophy, 3–4, 8–11, 18–19, 85, 141
Paul of Tarsus, 13, 26, 28, 98
Papus, 57, 59, 73, 141
Paracelsus, 84–85
Pentecost, 93–95
Pico della Mirandola, Giovanni, 2, 4–5
pietism, 83–86, 88, 139
Pike, Albert, 58–59, 141
Plato, 2
Plotinus, 2, 10
Poor People's Campaign (1968), 89–90, 92–93, 95–97, 99, 105
Poor People's Campaign: A National Call for Moral Revival (2018), 6n13, 93–94, 104n8, 105, 108, 112–14, 115n33, 116–17, 135, 139, 141, 143
poverty, 6, 46, 67, 92, 101, 105–106, 109, 112, 132
preferential option for the poor, 89–90
prisca theologica, 2, 4

Protestant Reformation, 1

Qabalah, 17, 21, 23, 25–51, 59, 66, 69, 73, 76, 78, 124, 128, 137–38, 141
  Binah, 34–37, 41, 50, 124
  Chesed, 37–40, 50
  Chokmah, 21, 33–37, 41, 44, 46, 50, 121
  Daath, 35–36, 49–51, 69, 124
  Geburah, 38–40, 50
  Hod, 44–49, 73, 75
  Kether, 20–1, 23, 32–34, 36, 41, 50, 59, 71, 74–75, 124, 126
  Malkuth, 41, 44, 49–51, 69, 73–74, 78, 122, 124, 126
  Netzach, 44–46, 48–49
  Tiphareth, 36, 40–45, 49, 51, 66, 69, 73–75, 77, 91n25, 124
  Tree of Life, 20, 26–51, 59, 69, 70–74, 99, 123–124
  Yesod, 44–49, 51

Recnartus, Frater, 18–19, 141
Regardie, Israel, 34, 36, 46–47, 49, 69, 141
Resurrection City, 91, 93, 99, 101
Rosicrucianism, 3–5, 8–9, 30, 40, 65, 69–70, 72, 84, 85–86, 134, 137–39, 143

Secret Chiefs, 70–72, 75–76, 86, 91, 100–101, 137
Second Vatican Council, 1
Segundo, Juan-Luis, 6, 61n22, 102–3, 109, 121, 141
Sölle, Dorothee, 7, 142
Schillebeeckx, Edward, 7, 12, 33–34, 59–60, 63, 103, 121–22, 128–30, 138, 141
Shrine of Wisdom, 17–18, 20, 143
Stringfellow, William, 27–30, 32, 57–59, 67, 138, 142

INDEX

Star of Bethlehem, 55–58, 66, 72, 75–77, 100, 126, 135
Snell, Merwin-Marie, 62, 64, 142
socialism, 22, 37n30
Spener, Philipp, 84
Srnicek, Nick, 105–107, 142
systemic racism, 6, 28, 39, 67, 92, 101, 104, 112, 132

Tarot, 31, 35–36, 39, 75, 77, 118, 132
Teilhard de Chardin, Pierre, 61–66, 68, 102–103, 121, 123, 126, 142
Thelema, 5, 11, 40, 76, 118–19, 121, 124–25
theurgy, 10, 19, 30, 56, 59–60, 72, 125, 142
Tiphareth. *See* Qabalah.
Traenker, Heinrich. *See* Recnartus, Frater.
Tree of Knowledge of Good and Evil, 50–51
Tree of Life. *See* Qabalah.
Trump, Donald, 132, 139

Union Theological Seminary, 6
Universal Brotherhood, 10n21, 18n3, 20, 62-64, 68n3, 122
Universal Order, 18n3

Universal Reformation, 1–4, 6–9, 68, 127, 134, 139

Virgin Mary, 35–36, 49, 63–65, 77–78, 124–25
von Eckartshausen, Karl, 85–89, 91, 101, 142

Waite, A.E., 22, 26, 60-61, 70–71, 86, 87n10, 97–98, 118, 142–43
Wessel-McCoy, Colleen, 90, 93, 95, 100
Western esotericism, 4, 6–8, 11, 65, 72, 85, 102, 114, 118, 131, 134–35, 138
Wicca, 118
Wildoak, Peregrin, 30–31, 143
Williams, Alex, 105–107, 142
Wink, Walter, 26–27, 29, 32, 140

Xenofeminism, 110–16, 119, 121, 140

Yates, Frances, 3, 143
Yeats, William Butler, 98–99, 143
Yesod. *See* Qabalah.

Zoroaster, 2

www.ingramcontent.com/pod-product-compliance
Lightning Source LLC
Chambersburg PA
CBHW072144160426
43197CB00012B/2240